"The angel of the LORD
encampeth round
about them that fear him,
and delivereth them"
(Psalms 34:7).

Angels All Around

The Present–day Ministry of Angels

BY MARILYN HICKEY

ANGELS ALL AROUND
The Present-day Ministry of Angels

P.O. Box 17340
Denver, Colorado 80217

ISBN 1-56441-000-5

Printed in the United States of America
All scriptures are quoted from the *King James* version of the Bible.

CONTENTS

Chapter One
ANGELS IN THE PAST

When Tommy Clark was only four years old, a bout with pneumonia left him near death. Doctors also told his mother that Tommy's heart was failing. The seriousness of Tommy's diagnosis was caused by the fact that he had been born with SMA—spinal muscular atrophy—a form of muscular dystrophy that destroys nerve cells. Tommy's condition appeared hopeless.

As he lay in his mother's arms, gasping for breath, Tommy looked up and said, ''Don't cry, Mommy.'' He then shared with her that an angel had appeared to him. ''There are hard times ahead,'' the angel told him, ''but things will be OK.''

Tommy survived that night's ordeal, and, in the three years since then, has experienced some ''hard times'' spoken of by the angel. But he has also enjoyed the love, joy, faith, and commitment of his parents who daily strive to make life as normal as possible for not only Tommy, but for Tommy's brother and sister—also diagnosed with SMA.

Many people today would cast doubt upon Tommy's angelic visitation. For them ''angels'' is a word found only in the Bible, and Tommy's experience is something to be explained away psychologically.

ANGELS—CREATED BEINGS

Are angels for real? The Bible says that angels are just as real as you and I. They are a race of superb beings with an important mission. They have a prominent place in Scripture, being mentioned over 300 times! We know from the psalms that God created the angels:

> *Praise ye him, all his angels: . . . for he* [God] *commanded, and they were created* (Psalms 148:2,5).

Angels, called ''sons of God'' by the author of the book of Job, were already present at the creation of the earth:

> *Where wast thou when I laid the foundations of the earth? declare, if thou hast understanding. When the morning stars sang together, and all the sons of God shouted for joy?* (Job 38:4,7).

The writer of Psalms 104 also confirms that angels were created *before* the earth:

> *Who maketh his angels spirits; his ministers a flaming fire: Who laid the foundations of the earth, that it should not be removed for ever* (Psalms 104:4,5).

We know little else about God's creation of the angels. Just as the writers of the Old and New Testaments assumed the existence of God, they also assumed the existence of angels. Like the wind, we may not always be able to see angels with our human eyes; but we can see their activity in our lives!

FALLEN ANGELS

Do you know how long angels were around before the earth was created? Nobody does; it could have been thousands of years. Satan was once one of God's ministering angels. In fact, he once ruled over the earth. At that time he was called *Lucifer, son of the morning*:

> *How art thou fallen from heaven, O Lucifer, son of the morning! how art thou cut down to the*

ground, which didst weaken the nations! (Isaiah 14:12).

Before his fall Satan was the anointed cherub (we'll learn more about cherubs later) who probably led angelic worship services in the Garden of Eden:

Thou hast been in Eden the garden of God; every precious stone was thy covering, . . . the workmanship of thy tabrets and of thy pipes was prepared in thee in the day that thou wast created. Thou art the anointed cherub that covereth; and I have set thee so: thou wast upon the holy mountain of God; . . . Thou wast perfect in thy ways from the day that thou wast created, till iniquity was found in thee (Ezekiel 28:13-15).

We know from Paul's letter to Timothy that Satan fell due to pride:

Not a novice, lest being lifted up with pride he fall into the condemnation of the devil (I Timothy 3:6).

The number of angels who *didn't* fall are said to be "innumerable" according to Hebrews 12:22. We are also told that one third of the angels (called "stars" in the book of Revelation) rebelled and fell with Satan:

And there appeared another wonder in heaven; and behold a great red dragon, having seven heads and ten horns, and seven crowns upon his heads. And his tail drew the third part of the stars of heaven, and did cast them to the earth: . . . (Revelations 12:3,4).

The Bible tells us that it was for *these* angels that God created hell:

Then shall he say also unto them on the left

hand, Depart from me, ye cursed, into everlasting fire, prepared for the devil and his angels (Matthew 25:41).

People sometimes ask me, "Marilyn, how can a loving God send someone to hell?" I always tell them, "God doesn't send anyone to hell; He created hell for the devil and his angels. People send themselves to hell by rejecting God's provision for salvation through Jesus Christ; don't blame God!"

ANGELS AND THEIR RANKS

Since Satan's fall constant warfare has been waged between the forces of evil and God. As in any warfare the "troops" on both sides of the battle are arranged in specific order. This angelic "chain of command" is seen in several places in the Bible. Paul mentions some general categories in his letter to the Ephesians:

Far above all principality, and power, and might, and dominion, and every name that is named, not only in this world, but also in that which is to come (Ephesians 1:21).

Not only is there war between good and evil angels, but Paul also tells us that *we* are involved in spiritual warfare against Satan and his angelic army:

For we wrestle not against flesh and blood, but against principalities, against powers, against the rulers of darkness of this world, against spiritual wickedness in high places (Ephesians 6:12).

How do we "wrestle" against these powerful spiritual beings? Our "fight" is *to stand* in the victory that Jesus has already won for us! Paul says that we are to "take" what Jesus has provided for our complete victory:

> *Wherefore take unto ye the whole armour of God, that ye may be able to withstand in the evil day, and having done all, to stand. Stand therefore, having your loins girt about with truth, and having on the breastplate of righteousness; And your feet shod with the preparation of the gospel of peace; Above all, taking the shield of faith, wherewith ye shall be able to quench all the fiery darts of the wicked. And take the helmet of salvation, and the sword of the Spirit, which is the word of God: Praying always with all prayer and supplication in the Spirit, . . .* (Ephesians 6:13-18).

You and I are in the angelic wrestling match at all times; we need to be ready for whatever the devil tries to throw at us. We need to have our loins girt about with truth. That means we're not into any false doctrines or flaky teachings. We must surround ourselves with the Word, the Word, the Word! We also need the breastplate of righteousness. We must examine ourselves and be sure we are walking in righteousness. Wherever there is sin or carnality, the devil has a way to get to us with the intent of destroying our testimony and our Christian walk.

Paul mentions the "shield of faith." If we don't stay in faith, we'll fall apart when pressure comes our way. We must also have on our helmet of salvation. We must be thinking God's thoughts and evaluating everything in light of God's Word. It's not, "What does the newspaper say about this situation?" or "What does Dan Rather say about this problem?" but "What does the Word of God say about this circumstance?''

One time a man asked me if I put on my armor each day. I said, ''No, I never take it off!'' We are always in some kind of conflict. We shouldn't wait until we're attacked by the enemy before putting on our armor.

ELECT ANGELS

Those angels who did not rebel with Satan are called ''elect'' angels:

> *I charge thee before God, and the Lord Jesus Christ, and the elect angels, that thou observe these things without preferring one before another, doing nothing by partiality* (I Timothy 5:21).

Remember, there are *two* elect angels for every *one* fallen angel. That means no matter how fierce the battle or how numerous the onslaughts of demonic activity, God's angels are *more than able* to come to your aid and to overcome the forces of darkness!

SERAPHIM

A very high-ranking order of angels is the *seraphim.* In Hebrew the name *seraphim* can mean ''burning, fiery'' or ''high, exalted.'' They are *burning* with zeal for the Lord. This *fiery* devotion to God may have resulted in their *high* and *exalted* position around the very throne of God! Isaiah is the only Biblical writer to mention these awesome creatures:

> *In the year that king Uzziah died I saw also the Lord sitting upon a throne, high and lifted up, and his train filled the temple. Above it stood the*

> *seraphims: each one had six wings; with twain he covered his face, and with twain he covered his feet, and with twain he did fly. And one cried unto another, and said, Holy, holy, holy, is the* LORD *of hosts: the whole earth is full of his glory* (Isaiah 6:1-3).

It appears that the seraphim supervise the praise of God. They proclaim His holiness. You and I can be *exalted* to God's throne room as we worship and lift up the holiness of the Lord in our lives.

CHERUBIM

The very first mention of an order of angels is the cherubim. We first see them guarding the entrance to the Garden of Eden after Adam and Eve had been expelled:

> *So he* [God] *drove out the man; and he placed at the east of the garden of Eden Cherubims, and a flaming sword which turned every way, to keep the way of the tree of life* (Genesis 3:24).

The next time the cherubim are mentioned is in connection with the furnishings of the Tabernacle. Here we read the first description of these angelic beings:

> *And thou shalt make two cherubims of gold, of beaten work shalt thou make them, in the two ends of the mercy seat. And the cherubims shall stretch forth their wings on high, covering the mercy seat with their wings, and their faces shall look one to another; toward the mercy seat shall the faces of the cherubims be* (Exodus 25:18,20).

Not all angels have wings, but the cherubim are said to have wings which cover the Mercy Seat. They seem to be closely connected with the presence of God and our redemption. Cherubim are mentioned by Ezekiel (chapter 10) and by John in his book of Revelation where they are called "living creatures" (Revelation 4).

ARCHANGEL

The Bible identifies only one angel as "chief," (which is the meaning of "arch"). Although there may be others (Gabriel may be one), *Michael* is the only archangel mentioned by name:

> *Yet Michael the archangel, when contending with the devil he disputed about the body of Moses, durst not bring against him a railing accusation, but said, The Lord rebuke thee* (Jude 9).

Michael means "who is like God?" We know from Daniel 10:13 that Michael is "... *one of the chief princes,* ...." These angelic authorities are constantly involved in warfare on behalf of God's people. Michael contended with the devil over the body of Moses, and we see him in battle with the devil again in the book of Revelation:

> *And there was war in heaven: Michael and his angels fought against the dragon; and the dragon fought and his angels, And prevailed not; neither was their place found any more in heaven* (Revelation 12:7,8).

Michael seems to have a special interest in the nation of Israel. During the Great Tribulation he will fight for the Jews:

> *And at that time shall Michael stand up, the great prince which standeth for the children of*

> *thy people: and there shall be a time of trouble, such as never was since there was a nation even to that same time: and at that time thy people shall be delivered, every one that shall be found written in the book* (Daniel 12:1).

GUARDIAN ANGELS

The writer to the Hebrews in the New Testament tells us that God has appointed angels to minister to the heirs of salvation:

> *Are they* [the angels] *not all ministering spirits, sent forth to minister for them who shall be heirs of salvation?* (Hebrews 1:14).

Are YOU an heir of salvation? Are YOU in the household of faith? Then you have special angels appointed just to YOU. Guardian angels show us just how much God loves us and how He is always doing everything to meet our needs, to prepare us, to assist us in all kinds of situations and circumstances.

Do these angels just hang around and watch what is going on? No! They are sent *to minister* to you. Psalms 34 tells us one of the things angels do for us:

> *The angel of the* LORD *encampeth round about them that fear him, and delivereth them* (Psalms 34:7).

What are the angels doing? They are there *to deliver* you whenever the situation calls for it. Psalms 91:11 tells us that angels are put in charge over us to keep us in all our ways. They are to take care of us and watch over us.

The Israelites had a guardian angel who helped them into the Promised Land; God said that the angel would fight for them:

> *And I* [God] *will send an angel before thee; and I will drive out the Canaanite, the Amorite, and the Hittite, and the Perizzite, the Hivite, and the Jebusite* (Exodus 33:2)

When we obey God, angels will fight for us. I don't like the pictures that some people paint of angels: long golden hair and harps in their hands. I don't think *all* angels carry harps around; I think they are very busy protecting us, guarding us.

Have you ever read the story of Paul and his voyage to Rome? At one point it looked as if the ship was going to capsize (Acts 27), but an angel came to Paul and told him that there would not be one life lost due to the storm. Where did that angel come from? It was Paul's guardian angel. Because Paul was on that ship, guardian angels were there; and everyone benefited from their presence!

Once when I was ministering at a prayer conference in Denver, I asked a friend to pick up my daughter Sarah after school (she was only five years old at the time). I told my friend where the bus would drop Sarah off and the time it would arrive. Unfortunately, the woman went to the wrong corner. Meanwhile Sarah had gotten off the bus and was waiting for the woman—but to no avail. Finally Sarah just headed off toward home, found the emergency key we had hidden, and let herself into the house.

Of course, when I heard what had happened, I thought, "I'll never do anything like that again; I'll always be there myself to make sure everything goes right." I continued to condemn myself until the Lord spoke up on the inside of me and said, "Marilyn, isn't Sarah all right? When you are about *My* business, I will be about *your* business."

Sarah's guardian angels had been watching over her. In fact, I had always prayed that angels would encamp around her and protect her in all her ways. The Lord had answered my prayers!

Some people think, "Well, I'll just sit back and do what I want; and my guardian angel will keep me and my loved ones from all harm." That's *not* the way it works. You and I have to do the praying before God can activate guardian angels.

That was certainly the experience of one woman who, as she tucked each of her children into bed, said a prayer of protection over them. Early the next morning, about 3:00 a.m., she was suddenly wide awake. Without knowing why, she ran down the hall to her daughter's room—just in time to stop the upper portion of the bunk bed from crashing down upon her daughter's head. Who had awakened this mother and alerted her to the disaster about to take place? Her child's guardian angel!

THE MINISTRY OF ANGELS—BIRTH ANNOUNCEMENTS

Being a guardian angel sounds like exciting work, but I think it would be equally exciting to be the bearer of God's good news of a forthcoming child in the life of any couple. The first "birth" announcement in the Bible is found in the book of Genesis. God had promised Abraham (Abram) and Sarah (Sarai) that they would have a child, but Sarah was a bit impatient. After being childless for years, Sarah allowed Abraham to father a child through her maid Hagar. But once Hagar knew she was pregnant, she despised Sarah and mocked her. Hagar eventually fled into the wilderness.

Imagine Hagar's distress. What would she eat? How would she survive? How would her baby ever be born? That's when God sent an angel to announce not only the fact that the baby would indeed be born, but also to prename the child:

> *And the angel of the LORD said unto her, Behold, thou art with child, and shalt bear a son, and shalt call his name Ishmael; because the LORD hath heard thy affliction* (Genesis 16:11).

Perhaps it was the very same angel who announced to Abraham and Sarah that they would have a child within a year's time:

> *And they said unto him, Where is Sarah thy wife? And he said, Behold, in the tent. And he said, I will certainly return unto thee according to the time of life; and, lo, Sarah thy wife shall have a son. And Sarah heard it in the tent door, which was behind him* (Genesis 18:9,10).

Although Sarah laughed at the announcement, the following year she gave birth to Isaac, which means "laughter." God had the last laugh!

Another birth announcement was made to a childless couple in fulfillment of Jacob's prophecy over his children before he died (Genesis 49). Jacob said that Dan would "judge his people." When we read the book of Judges, we find that only ONE judge came from the tribe of Dan!

The Bible calls the mother of this judge a "woman of God"; and while she was in the field, an angel appeared to her:

> *And the angel of the LORD appeared unto the woman, and said unto her, Behold now, thou art*

> *barren, and bearest not: but thou shalt conceive, and bear a son* (Judges 13:3).

When she told her husband about the angel and his message, her husband prayed and asked the Lord to send the angel back so they could receive instruction on how to raise their baby! I love the attitude of that father; and you know what? The angel *did* come back and gave the couple instruction for raising SAMSON, one of the mightiest judges of Israel!

Evidently God thinks that birth announcements are important; in the New Testament we read about how none other than *Gabriel* announced the birth and name of John the Baptist to his father:

> *And there appeared unto him an angel of the Lord standing on the right side of the altar of incense. And when Zacharias saw him, he was troubled, and fear fell upon him. But the angel said unto him, Fear not, Zacharias: for thy prayer is heard; and thy wife Elisabeth shall bear thee a son, and thou shalt call his name John* (Luke 1:11-13).

Six months later Gabriel's assignment sent him back to the same vicinity—only this time he had the privilege of announcing the birth of Jesus to a virgin from Nazareth:

> *And in the sixth month the angel Gabriel was sent from God unto a city of Galilee, named Nazareth, To a virgin espoused to a man whose name was Joseph, of the house of David; and the virgin's name was Mary. And the angel said unto her, Fear not, Mary: for thou hast found favour with God. And, behold, thou shalt conceive in thy womb, and bring forth a son, and*

shalt call his name JESUS (Luke 1:26,27,30,31).

You might be thinking, ''My, isn't that nice; angels are such sweet things. They kind of fly around and bring birth announcements and name babies.'' Yes, they *do* bring birth announcements, but don't let that fool you! Angels are mighty warriors who make ''Star Wars'' look like a picnic! In the next chapter, we'll look into the angelic warfare that occurred back in Daniel's day; and then we'll look ahead to the cataclysmic battle that is yet to be fought by angels in heaven!

Chapter Two
ANGELIC CONFLICT

Do you know that on any given day there are at least a dozen different wars being fought somewhere in the world? Our news media does a good job of informing us of the major "hot spots"—like the Middle East and South Africa. There is one war, however, that I know you haven't heard about on ABC, NBC, or CBS. This war can't be seen with the human eye; there are no sounds of artillery, no crack of rifles firing, no bombs being dropped, or missiles being launched. Yet this war is by far the largest conflict ever waged!

The Bible gives us glimpses of this war in several places; it is, as the apostle John calls it, a "war in the heavenlies." The "troops" on each side are mighty angelic beings, and the stakes involved affect the status of nations and the answers to millions of prayers offered up by God's people throughout the world.

This angelic battle has been raging for thousands of years. The book of Job (thought by many to be the first written book of the Old Testament) pulls aside the curtain of heaven and gives us a vivid glimpse of the spirit realm. By comparing, combining, and contrasting other portions of the Bible, we can gain a better understanding of what the apostle Paul calls "*. . . principalities, . . . powers, . . . rulers of the darkness of this world, . . . spiritual wickedness in high places*" (Ephesians 6:12).

In the first chapter of Job we read about Satan and his band of fallen angels appearing before the Lord:

> *Now there was a day when the sons of God came to present themselves before the* L*ORD*, *and*

> *Satan came also among them* (Job 1:6).

We know from Job 38:7 that "the sons of God" mentioned here refers to angels. Why were Satan and the other fallen angels standing before God? The answer to that question probably goes back to God's judgment upon the devil and the angels who followed him in his rebellion:

> *Then shall he say also unto them on the left hand, Depart from me, ye cursed, into everlasting fire, prepared for the devil and his angels* (Matthew 25:41).

Satan no doubt objected to God's punishment, saying, "That's not fair! I didn't really have any other choice. Nobody would serve You *freely*, so why punish me? It's not my fault You created me this way! God, You're unjust!"

The devil's accusation may have actually prompted God to create Adam and Eve with a free will to disprove Satan's claim! Now, every time a man or woman *freely* decides to obey and worship God, Satan's objection is proved wrong.

To prove Satan wrong, God gave him liberty to remove the benefits that Job's righteous living had brought to him. Satan was limited in what he could do to Job, but the book of Job gives us a clear picture of the hatred Satan has for mankind, especially those who freely love and serve God.

Christians today are under similar attacks by Satan and his demon spirits. We may not always have a "pat" answer to life's tragedies, but we know from the Bible that man's sin and Satan's hatred of Christians combine to produce horrifying circumstances where the outcome depends on spiritual warfare in the unseen realm.

SPIRITUAL WARFARE TODAY

I want to share with you a modern-day Job story—a story of Satan coming to steal, kill, and destroy in the life of someone who freely loves God. You probably have heard similar accounts from Christians who were under attack; Job's suffering is not unique! But unless we realize the spirit activity behind many physical events, we cannot hope to fight back at the source—and win! Listen as a personal acquaintance of mine shares her testimony:

> "One day late in January 1972—I'll never forget what a sunny, gorgeous day it was—I arrived home from a most wonderful time of skiing with a friend. The kids said some man had been calling all afternoon. Before I could get my coat off, the phone rang. When I answered it, a man said, 'This is the morgue. We have your husband down here, and we need you to come over and identify the body.'
>
> "I said, 'You're lying to me . . . this is a terrible joke!'
>
> "'Lady,' he said, 'this is no joke; just call the police.'
>
> "Sure enough, the police verified that my husband had been shot. Several neighbors went with me. When we arrived I saw my husband (and the father of my four children) full of bullet holes . . . not cleaned up . . . blood all over and bottles hanging with tubes running it seemed everywhere.
>
> "The police said some 16-year-old kids shot my husband and that, 'This thing happens all the

> time in that area of town.'
>
> "I remember sitting on the divan with the four kids, all crying . . . one boy in the sixth grade, one boy in the fifth grade, and another boy and girl in the first grade. I was absolutely numb. I knew we had no money, or very little; and I didn't know how in the world I could raise four kids."

The murder of this woman's husband was followed, within a three-year period, by the death of her mother and open-heart surgery for one of her children! Here was a woman under attack! "How on earth did she survive all that?" you might ask. I'll tell you: she learned about the spiritual forces at work behind the scene, and she learned to fight a spiritual fight. It didn't happen overnight, but over a period of time she turned her attention away from the physical tragedies around her and focused her thoughts on the presence of Jesus and the power of His blood to heal and to make whole.

Don't you know that the atmosphere around her must have been charged with clashing angels! Satan's spirits of depression were constantly vying for supremacy over her mind, while God's holy angels sought to overcome thoughts of defeat, loneliness, and despair planted by the devil.

Today, this woman says, "God is merciful and full of grace. God's grace brought me through, and I am seeing His glory!"

How about YOU? In some area of your life or in the life of a loved one, there is an angelic battle going on in the unseen realm of the spirit. God's angels are on YOUR side, fighting their way through demonic spirits who constantly tell you to give up. Don't give in to despair! Don't struggle in the flesh to get the answers you desire. PRAY, PRAY, PRAY to see the spiritual aspect of your conflict. And know that Satan's angelic army has only *limited access* to work against you. Know that God's angels outnumber Satan's 2 to 1, and they are fighting to see you win the victory in every area of your life.

ANGELIC INFLUENCE OVER NATIONS

Angels are not only concerned with your *personal* affairs, they are also very much involved with the affairs of *nations*. Nowhere is this more clearly seen than in the Old Testament book of Daniel.

Daniel was a praying saint! He had been taken captive to Babylon when he was just a teenager. Daniel was someone who *prayed the Word*. He knew from reading Jeremiah's writing that the Jews were to remain captive in Babylon for 70 years:

> *And this whole land shall be a desolation, and an astonishment; and these nations shall serve the king of Babylon seventy years* (Jeremiah 25:11).

When the 70 years were up, Daniel no doubt began praying for God to answer Jeremiah's prophecy. In Daniel 10 we read about Daniel's 21 days of fasting and prayer:

> *In those days I Daniel was mourning three full weeks. I ate no pleasant bread, neither came flesh nor wine in my mouth, neither did I anoint myself at all, till three whole weeks were fulfilled* (Daniel 10:2,3).

I believe the narrative that begins in verse five describes

a visitation of the Lord Jesus Christ to Daniel. When Daniel experienced his great vision, he lost all strength to stand and fell with his face on the ground. Then the angel Gabriel appeared to Daniel:

And, behold, an hand touched me, which set me upon my knees and upon the palms of my hands. And he said unto me, O Daniel, a man greatly beloved, understand the words that I speak unto thee, and stand upright: for unto thee am I now sent. And when he had spoken this word unto me, I stood trembling (Daniel 10:10,11).

Beginning with Daniel 10:12 we have the curtain of heaven pulled back once again, and we are given a very intimate view of what happens between heaven and earth when men and women pray. In this account we see the *star wars* that literally go on in the spirit realm. The outcome of these angelic conflicts, as we shall see, affect the destiny of nations!

Does God take notice of the saints' prayers? Absolutely! Notice closely what the angel Gabriel told Daniel:

Then said he [the angel] *unto me, Fear not, Daniel: for from the first day that thou didst set thine heart to understand, and to chasten thyself before thy God, thy words were heard, and I am come for thy words. But the prince of the kingdom of Persia withstood me one and twenty days: but, lo, Michael, one of the chief princes, came to help me; and I remained there with the kings of Persia* (Daniel 10:12,13).

Daniel's prayers were heard the very first day they were uttered; but there were 21 days of angelic warfare before Michael, another of God's mighty angels, came to the rescue of Gabriel. It took both of them to break through the satanic blockade that kept Gabriel from appearing before Daniel with the assurance of answered prayer. So we see that there is a spirit world very much involved in the affairs of men and the nations which are upon this earth.

Satan is called the *"prince of the power of the air"*:

> *Wherein in time past ye walked according to the course of this world, according to the prince of the power of the air, the spirit that now worketh in the children of disobedience* (Ephesians 2:2).

Jesus also called him the *"prince of this world"*:

> *Hereafter I will not talk much with you: for the prince of this world cometh, and hath nothing in me"* (John 14:30).

There is no question that Satan has an organized government—principalities and powers, rulers of darkness, and spiritual wickedness in high places. I believe that the prince of Persia is Satan's leader of wickedness in high places. Undoubtedly high-ranking evil spirits are appointed over nations, and the prayers of God's people affect the outcome of their evil assignments!

In verse 20 of Daniel chapter 10 we read that Gabriel was to return to fight with the prince of Persia:

> *Then said he* [Gabriel], *Knowest thou wherefore I come unto thee? and now will I return to fight with the prince of Persia: and when I am gone forth, lo, the prince of Grecia shall come* (Daniel 10:20).

There was to be more fighting for Gabriel on his way back to the throne of God! Once Gabriel was gone, the "prince of Greece" (the evil angelic ruler in charge of the affairs of the Grecian Empire) would arrive on the scene to guide Alexander the Great in his amazing conquest of the Medo-Persian Empire in just 13 years.

These verses give us insight into the powerful control such principalities and rulers of darkness may exercise over nations and national issues. The ruling prince of Persia, an evil angel, attempted to keep the captive Israelites from returning to their homeland. But the prayers of God's people resulted in an angelic battle that loosed Satan's grip over the secular powers of that day. The result was freedom for the Jews to return home—just as God had promised 70 years earlier!

THE DEVIL AND KING DAVID

What's the easist way to destroy a nation? Go after its leaders! That's just what Satan attempted to do when he used his subtlety to "provoke" King David:

> *And Satan stood up against Israel, and provoked David to number Israel* (I Chronicles 21:1).

Notice that Satan was coming against *Israel* by attacking its king. David was taken in by Satan's idea to take a census of the nation. David's military advisor, Joab, objected to what David wanted to do: "David," he said, "I don't have a good feeling about this. You're numbering Israel to find out how big your army is. God has always protected us, and you're trying to put confidence in numbers instead of the Lord."

David was in the middle of an angelic conflict. Unfortunately, he listened to the wrong voice. God was not pleased:

> *And God was displeased with this thing;*

therefore he smote Israel. And David said unto God, I have sinned greatly, because I have done this thing: but now, I beseech thee, do away the iniquity of thy servant; for I have done very foolishly (I Chronicles 21:7,8).

David knew he had blown it. Notice that he didn't say, "The devil made me do it!" He took responsibility for his sin. Yes, the devil and his angels will use any and every means to tempt God's people to sin, but God has given us the means to say "No!" to every temptation. We can call on the holy angels to fight on our behalf; we have prayer, we have the Word, we have the baptism of the Holy Spirit, and we have the local church.

Are you in a place of leadership? Are you responsible for your family, your office, your Sunday school class, or some other group? Then Satan is out to bring down that group through you by provoking you to sin. You are one point of focus in the great angelic warfare that continues silently in the spiritual realm. Remember that God and His angels are on your side; use all the spiritual weapons that are available to guarantee your victory!

WHEN THE WALL CAME TUMBLIN' DOWN

Are there evil angelic forces seeking to influence government leaders today? I believe there are; and I believe that, just as in David's day and in Daniel's day, the prayers of God's people greatly affect their control over nations today.

Do you remember when you heard the "unbelievable" news that the Berlin Wall was being demolished? Most people never thought that such a thing would happen in their lifetime. The secular news media gave us the "facts" surrounding this joyous event, but the world was never given the *spiritual* events that led up to the amazing decline of communism in Eastern Europe.

Sometimes we forget that, while a government may be officially "atheistic," the Church of Jesus Christ is still alive in every part of the world! Christians throughout Europe have never stopped praying *"For kings, and for all that are in authority; . . . "* (I Timothy 2:2).

Those prayers enable God's angels to battle the evil principalities in charge of cities and nations. Just months before the dismantling of the Berlin Wall, Billy Graham held an evangelistic campaign in Germany. Hundreds of churches were involved, with thousands of Christians praying daily for the success of the gospel in this part of the world. Their prayers, together with the prayers of Christians all over the world, were the unseen force that brought the Berlin Wall down. Praise the Lord! We need to continue praying for nations and their leaders; God's angels are sent into action from the very first day of our intercession. As we continue to pray for nations, God will continue to do the "impossible"!

MICHAEL AND THE BODY OF MOSES

The little book of Jude in the New Testament gives us another glimpse of angelic warfare. The half-brother of Jesus mentions the archangel Michael "contending" with the devil over the body of Moses:

> *Yet Michael the archangel, when contending with the devil he disputed about the body of Moses, durst not bring against him a railing*

> *accusation, but said, The Lord rebuke thee* (Jude 9).

Deuteronomy 34:5, 6 tells us of the death of Moses and how God buried him in an unknown location. The devil evidently thought he had some claim to the body of Moses. The archangel Michael thought otherwise, disputed with the devil over Moses' body, and finally stepped out of the way to allow the Lord to exercise authority over the devil.

Are you a Christian? Do you have the life of God residing on the inside of you? Then God and His holy angels have a vital interest in everything about you! When I was in junior high school, the girls who felt extra special were the ones who had several boys "fighting" for their attention. You and I can feel *extra special,* not because of some fleshly, silly attention from the opposite sex, but because God's angels are fighting for us. How can we help our angels in their efforts? We can stay in God's Word, stay in prayer, and stay in faith.

THE COMING WAR IN THE HEAVENLIES

According to the twelfth chapter of the book of Revelation, John saw a "great wonder" in heaven: a woman gave birth to a "man child" who is to rule all the nations with a rod of iron. This man child is "caught up" to God's throne to escape Satan. This is a picture of the Rapture:

> *For the Lord himself shall descend from heaven with a shout, with the voice of the archangel, and with the trump of God: and the dead in Christ shall rise first: Then we which are alive and*

remain shall be caught up together with them in the clouds, to meet the Lord in the air: and so shall we ever be with the Lord (I Thessalonians 4:16,17).

The resurrection of the saved dead and the Rapture of the living saints will be a tremendous undertaking, and the powers of the heavens will be involved. When the Church is caught up, a lot of things will happen. Remember, there will be millions arriving in heaven at the same time. This ruling class will take over with Jesus and will share His throne.

When the Church arrives in heaven, it spells the downfall of Satan. Since Satan has always occupied the area between the earth and heaven, he is in a good place to "devour" the child as soon as it is born. But God will shake him out of the heavenlies:

Whose voice then shook the earth: but now he hath promised, saying, Yet once more I shake not the earth only, but also heaven (Hebrews 12:26).

Michael will stand up for the raptured saints; he will war against Satan just as he warred against Satan for Moses' body:

And there was war in heaven: Michael and his angels fought against the dragon; and the dragon fought and his angels, And prevailed not; neither was their place found any more in heaven (Revelation 12:7,8).

Satan is going to do everything he can to stop the Rapture; that's why it is a *secret* rapture. God wants a surprise attack on Satan. Because Satan is the prince of the power of the air, the rapture of millions of saints and their trip through the air will cleanse it from all demonic influence. Satan is cast down to earth following the Rapture. He knows his time is short at that point, so he begins a terrible persecution of those saved following the Rapture.

These "angelic wars" will be greater than any "Star Wars" conceived by man! You and I will be part of that great war which results in Satan being cast down to earth.

Can you see now why Satan's angels are very much interested in YOU? God is preparing you now to be a part of His end-time plans. But Satan wants to neutralize you and cause you to miss the Rapture. Don't you let him! Pray, read the Word, stay in fellowship with other Christians, and build your faith up by being active in a local church. Begin to reign and rule with Christ NOW in preparation for that day when you are caught up to His throne to rule the nations.

Chapter Three

ANGELS IN JESUS' LIFE

Have you ever dreamed about having a servant? When I was a little girl, I sometimes thought, "Wouldn't it be nice to have my own servant to wash these dishes for me! If I had my own personal servant, I wouldn't have to do *any* of my chores!"

Do you know that Jesus has His own personal servant? He does, but I'm sure that His ministering angel isn't concerned with doing dishes or making beds! In fact, the last book of the Bible tells us that Jesus sent His own personal angel to be an *interpreter* so that the apostle John could understand the many terrifying and mysterious symbols that are part of the book of Revelation:

> *The Revelation of Jesus Christ, which God gave unto him, to shew unto his servants things which must shortly come to pass; and he sent and signified it by his angel unto his servant John* (Revelation 1:1).

John was about to receive a vision that included strange beasts, locusts, a harlot riding on a beast, a dragon, and much more. Jesus' angel explained to John the meaning of these strange symbols:

> *And the angel said unto me, Wherefore didst thou marvel? I will tell thee the mystery of the woman, and of the beast that carrieth her, which hath the seven heads and ten horns* (Revelation 17:7).

Angels are often used as interpreters in the Bible. Zechariah received several visions from the Lord, and he asked an angel to explain what they meant:

Then lifted I up mine eyes, and saw, and behold four horns. And I said unto the angel that talked with me, What be these? And he answered me, These are the horns which have scattered Judah, Israel, and Jerusalem (Zechariah 1:18,19).

Ministering spirits are *practical.* They're not just flying around and playing games. They're involved in "big time" things like angelic warfare, and they're also involved, one-on-one, with believers to help them understand the Scriptures.

ANGELS, MARY, JOSEPH, AND JESUS

We've already seen how the angel Gabriel announced the birth of Jesus to His mother Mary. The gospel of Matthew tells us that an angel also appeared to Joseph after he heard the news that Mary was expecting. Imagine his feelings when he first received the news! Evidently he was a little skeptical of Mary's story and was considering ending their engagement.

An angel appeared to Joseph while he was thinking about what to do:

But while he thought on these things, behold, the angel of the Lord appeared unto him in a dream, saying, Joseph, thou son of David, fear not to take unto thee Mary thy wife: for that which is conceived in her is of the Holy Ghost (Matthew 1:20).

We're not told the name of the angel who appeared to Joseph; perhaps it was Gabriel, or perhaps another angel was assigned to speak to the one who would become the earthly father of Jesus. Regardless of who the angel was, it is easy to see that this was certainly no ordinary baby about to be born. An angel had appeared to Mary to announce Jesus' birth, and an angel appeared to Joseph to put his fears to rest.

''Fear not'' is something Jesus told His disciples over and over again. ''Fear not'' is something God is constantly telling His children when things look a little scary.

A woman I'll call ''Helen'' was heartbroken and overwhelmed when the doctors told her that Billy, her six-week old son, was blind.

''I didn't have the words to pray. I felt such sadness for my little Billy. Then I began to wonder how in the world I would ever be able to raise a blind child—it seemed impossible at the time.''

Helen's friends at church began to pray, and Helen began to read and meditate in the Word. One scripture that came to mean a lot to her was Deuteronomy 33:27, '' . . . *and underneath are the everlasting arms:* . . . .''

One day when Helen took Billy for a checkup, a stranger in the waiting room began to chat with her. When Helen shared some of her fears about raising a blind child, the stranger said sweetly, ''Don't be afraid . . . 'underneath are the everlasting arms'!''

For Helen, those words '' . . . were like a message of confirmation from heaven; they just seemed to melt away all my fears.'' Billy's condition didn't change, *but Helen's did.* She became confident that God would help her meet the challenges that each day would bring. Today Billy is an adult; he's finished college and is employed.

Did God arrange for an angel to be in that waiting room on the day of Helen's visit? I don't know. But the stranger's message of ''Fear not'' was the same message that calmed the fears of Joseph and the disciples of Jesus. And it's the same message that can change YOUR worst fears into faith—faith that will work miracles in your own life and in the lives of your family.

ANGELS AND SHEPHERDS

''Fear not'' is also the message that angels spoke to shepherds at the time of Jesus' birth:

> *And there were in the same country shepherds abiding in the field, keeping watch over their flock by night. And, lo, the angel of the Lord came upon them, and the glory of the Lord shone round about them: and they were sore afraid. And the angel said unto them, Fear not: . . .* (Luke 2:8-10).

Angels are awesome creatures; some appear as ordinary men while others may be 8-10 feet tall! There must have been something quite unusual about the angel who appeared to the shepherds. These were rugged men who were used to living outdoors. They fought off wolves and bears to protect their flock. There was also the constant danger of robbers roaming the countryside in search of anyone with something of value. Sheep would have been a prime target for thieves.

No, it couldn't have been an ordinary-looking man who appeared to the shepherds; it was the mighty ''angel of the Lord.'' His appearance frightened the shepherds so much that the first thing the angel did was to calm their fears!

Next the angel announced the birth of Jesus to the shepherds:

> *. . . behold, I bring you good tidings of great joy, which shall be to all people. For unto you is born this day in the city of David a Saviour, which is Christ the Lord* (Luke 2:10,11).

This angel was not alone. He was "suddenly" joined by a "multitude" of heaven's angelic army:

> *And suddenly there was with the angel a multitude of the heavenly host praising God, and saying, Glory to God in the highest, and on earth peace, good will toward men* (Luke 2:13,14).

Angels were very much involved with the entrance of our Savior into this world! As we've already seen, they announced the birth of Jesus' forerunner John the Baptist, announced Jesus' birth to Mary, calmed the fears of Joseph, and proclaimed Christ's birth to some shepherds in the hills of Judea. There is no such thing as "unemployment" for angels!

ANGELS AS PROTECTORS

There doesn't seem to be any limit to the assignments given to angels. They fight their way through evil principalities to bring believers answers to prayers; they make birth announcements; and they encourage believers in the faith. In addition to those duties, angels act as *protectors* of God's people. An angelic message to Joseph protected the life of Jesus when He was still a helpless baby:

> *. . . the angel of the Lord appeareth to Joseph in a dream, saying, Arise, and take the young child and his mother, and flee into Egypt; and be*

> *thou there until I bring thee word: for Herod will seek the young child to destroy him* (Matthew 2:13).

We would quite naturally expect angels to protect the life of God's only Son, but do you know that God's angels are all around YOU for YOUR protection? They most certainly are!

One night a family had just returned from a church supper. As they readied themselves for bed, the smoke detector sounded. The father made a dash for the area of the house where the alarm was located. As he came within sight of the alarm, the piercing siren stopped. There was no trace of smoke, and he commented to his wife about the strange occurrence when he got back to their bedroom.

"Oh, dear!" his wife said with a shocked expression. "That reminds me that I didn't turn the coffee pot off before we left the church!"

Her husband drove back to the church, returning 20 minutes later to say that she had, indeed, left the coffee pot on the burner. It had boiled dry and had started to smoke.

Was it just coincidence that their smoke alarm sounded and jogged the wife's memory about the coffee pot? I don't think so. I think a protecting angel set the alarm off to save that church from burning down. God's angels are practical, and nothing in the Christian life is "mere coincidence."

God's protecting angels are always around us, helping to keep us safe. When we get up in the morning and drive or take the bus to work, angels are guarding our steps in ways we may never know. The prophet Jeremiah had real insight into God's constant protection over our lives. *"It is of the LORD'S mercies,"* the prophet wrote, *that we are not consumed, because his compassions fail not"* (Lamentations 3:22).

Jeremiah went on to write about God's great faithfulness. When is the last time you expressed your thankfulness to the Lord for His compassion, faithfulness, and protection over your life and the lives of your loved ones? You don't have to wait for the smoke alarm to sound or for a close call in traffic. The time to thank the Lord for angelic protection is EACH AND EVERY DAY!

I have known the protection of angels on many occasions. One time, as my husband Wally and I were taking a group to the Holy Land, we stopped for two days in Rome for a little sightseeing. It was raining the day we were visiting the various beautiful Roman cathedrals, and a group of us stood on a corner waiting for an opportune moment to dash across one of those busy Roman streets. There were many little cars beeping as they rushed pell-mell down that bustling avenue.

Seeing what I thought was an opportunity to cross, I made a dash for it. Too late, I saw a city bus turn the corner—and I was in its path! The bus screeched to a halt; but not before it hit my right hip, tossing me in the air until I landed on the wet street. Everyone jumped out of the bus talking in what sounded to me like excited gibberish—I didn't understand a word of Italian.

My first thought was, "I wonder if I can stand up?" Timidly I tried my legs and stood up with no difficulty. I examined myself, felt no pain, and to my surprise I found that my coat was not even wet although I had landed on the dampened pavement. Neither was there even so much as a run in my nylons.

Later, I looked at my right hip; and there was not even a bruise! We had claimed the promises of God for His protection during our trip, and the Lord had certainly answered in a miraculous way. I'm glad angels are as fast as the wind, because an angel must have descended fast that day to pick me up from the path of that large city bus.

JESUS, TEMPTATION, AND ANGELS

Sometimes, when we think about Jesus in His divinity, we might think, "Why in the world would Jesus need angels? He was (and is) almighty God!" But Jesus gave up His rights as equal with the Father when He came to earth in human flesh:

> *Who,* [Jesus] *being in the form of God, thought it not robbery to be equal with God: But made himself of no reputation, and took upon him the form of a servant, and was made in the likeness of men* (Philippians 2:6,7).

While He was on this earth, Jesus, as man, was totally dependent upon His heavenly Father. And it was the Father Who sent angels to minister to Jesus. At the very beginning of His public ministry, Jesus went into the wilderness to fast and pray. At the end of 40 days of fasting the devil came to Him (wouldn't you know that the devil would wait until AFTER Jesus went without food for 40 days!) and tempted Him. Satan tempted Jesus by quoting (actually MISquoting) from Psalms 91 in regard to the ministry of angels:

> *. . . If thou be the Son of God, cast thyself down from hence: For it is written, He shall give his*

angels charge over thee, to keep thee: And in their hands they shall bear thee up, lest at any time thou dash thy foot against a stone (Luke 4:9-11).

Even the devil knew about the protection provided by angels for God's elect—and especially His only begotten Son. But Jesus knew that it wasn't proper to tempt God into activating angels when there wasn't a genuine need for their help:

And Jesus answering said unto him, It is said, Thou shalt not tempt the Lord thy God (Luke 4:12).

Seeing that he was unsuccessful in tempting Jesus, the devil left Him. I think this was a "pressure" time for Jesus. These were very real temptations for Jesus. The Bible wouldn't record them if they were just some light, fluffy, passing thoughts. Angels are sent to minister to us during the "pressure" times of life.

Is this a "pressure" time for you? Then be assured that God's angels are present to minister to your needs. It was Matthew who recorded the ministry of angels to Jesus following His temptation:

Then the devil leaveth him, and, behold, angels came and ministered unto him (Matthew 4:11).

Did the angels bring Jesus food? Did they offer Him encouragement? Did they speak to Him of His coming ministry? We're not told *what* kind of ministry these angels performed, but Luke does tell us the *result* of that angelic ministry:

And Jesus returned in the power of the Spirit into Galilee: and there went out a fame of him through all the region round about (Luke 4:14).

Would you like more ''power of the Spirit'' in your life? Then look to the Lord to provide angelic ministry as you fast, pray, and seek His will. Keep in mind the words of Paul concerning the temptations you face:

> *There hath no temptation taken you but such as is common to man: but God is faithful, who will not suffer you to be tempted above that ye are able; but will with the temptation also make a way to escape, that ye may be able to bear it* (I Corinthians 10:13).

God's angels will minister to you and cause you to be victorious over any situation that tempts you to doubt God's goodness and provision. Use the Word, as Jesus did, to send the devil packing!

ANGELS AND THE LATTER MINISTRY OF JESUS

The next time we read of direct angelic ministry in Jesus' life is in the Garden of Gethsemane. Jesus went into the garden to pray. He called Peter, James, and John to go in and pray with Him. Jesus knew that He was in a spiritual battle. From reading the gospel of Luke, we can see that there was a tremendous temptation for Jesus to look for a way to avoid going to the Cross to pay for the sins of the world.

Jesus prayed, ''Father, I know I have to go to the Cross; but if there is any other way, ... But not My will—Your will be done.'' There was a real temptation to find another solution to the problem of sin. Don't think, ''Well, Jesus was the Son of God so of course it was easy for Him to go to the Cross.'' No, no, no!! Jesus went to the Cross as the *Son of Man.* As a *man* He was genuinely tempted to skip the Cross—divinity can't be tempted, but man can be tempted.

Peter, James, and John were with Jesus on that night of agony. Jesus probably brought them along to pray with Him and to encourage Him. But what happened? The disciples fell asleep! Some help they were!

But Jesus did receive encouragement as He prayed alone on the night of His betrayal:

> *And there appeared an angel unto him from heaven, strengthening him* (Luke 22:43).

Have you ever asked a friend to pray for you? Have you ever been in a crisis situation where you felt you needed the strengthening of another church member? Have they ever let you down? Then you know how Jesus felt when the hour of His greatest need arose and His own disciples slept rather than prayed!

Yes, we need the prayers and support of our pastors and other members of the Body of Christ; but if others fail us, God can send His angels to minister to us. I know a man (I'll call him Louis) who experienced the ministry of angels not only when others prayed for him but also at a time when no one knew that he needed angelic intervention.

Early in his life Louis lived through a very turbulent time in his country's history. One day Louis was out playing football, and he saw Jesus—he had a vision of Jesus Christ—and he was born again. About that time Louis' country went to war; and for some reason, he was imprisoned. Other Christians knew about his confinement and began to pray for him. There was a whole group of Christians who prayed day and night. They knew that their friend had been imprisoned illegally and that he might be killed at any time.

One night a man dressed as a military police officer came and unlocked the door of Louis' cell. He said, "Follow me." Louis noticed that as he followed this "man," some unusual things happened. The man never unlocked the other doors before him; they just popped open. The man had unlocked *his* cell, but he did not unlock the doors on the way out of the prison. When they finally got outside, the man said, "Go home"; then he disappeared. Louis realized that he had seen an angel of the Lord!

Louis left his country, came to America, and began to share his experiences with small groups all over the nation. One night he was in Colorado; and the weather was very, very cold and snowy. He was on one side of a mountain ministering, and the next day he was to minister to a church on the other side of the mountain. All the weather forecasts said the roads were impassable; but Louis knew that if he didn't drive over the mountain that night, he wouldn't be able to minister the next day and he would have to cancel his meeting.

Louis believed that the Lord wanted him to go so he prayed, "Lord, I believe You want me to minister at that church tomorrow; so I believe you will protect me and take care of me." A few minutes after he started driving, Louis spotted a hitchhiker. It had never been his custom to pick up hitchhikers, but the Lord spoke to him and told him to pick up the hitchhiker (please don't do this unless you're *sure* the Lord has told you to do it!).

It was dark outside and snowing; the man was bundled up for the cold. Louis began to witness to the man, but the man began to speak to him about things in the future. Louis was quite aware that something supernatural was going on!

When the car passed under a highway light Louis got a good look at the hitchhiker. It was the same man who had led him through the prison and released him! Louis said, "You're an angel of the Lord!" When he said that, the man disappeared. Louis was on the other side of the mountain and drove safely into the town where he was to minister.

The first time Louis encountered the angel, believers were praying for supernatural intervention. God answered their prayers and sent his angel. But there was no one praying for Louis the night he decided to drive through the snow on the icy mountain pass. He was all alone. But God sent an angel to minister to him and guide him safely to his destination, and God will do the same for you if you request the ministry of angels.

Does it seem as if you have been left alone to fend for yourself? Are you going through a personal "Gethsemane" where those you depended upon have let you down? Then set yourself to pray and expect God's ministering angels to strengthen you just as they strengthened Jesus in the Garden of Gethsemane. If Jesus could face the agonies of the Cross through the help of ministering angels, then YOU can face any temptation or difficulty that lies before you!

JESUS AND THE 72,000 ANGELS

Believe it or not, people used to argue about how many angels could fit on the head of a pin! Such silly speculation does nothing to build our faith or give us courage in spiritual warfare. But something Jesus said just before He was arrested in the Garden of Gethsemane can give us a glimpse of the angelic power that is available for believers:

> *Thinkest thou that I cannot now pray to my Father, and he shall presently give me more than twelve legions of angels?* (Matthew 26:53).

A Roman legion was composed of 6,000 soldiers; so 12 legions of angels would be 72,000 mighty, heavenly warriors! When you remember that ONE angel killed 185,000 of Assyria's finest fighting men (II Kings 19:35), you begin to comprehend the power at Jesus' disposal had He wanted to oppose those who put Him on the Cross!

Sometimes it seems that Christianity is weak and powerless in the face of the liberal media and the secular humanists who have become so very influential in our government. But wait! It only *looked* like Jesus was powerless when the Roman soldiers arrested Him and brought Him to trial. Jesus knew, however, that nothing could hinder God's ultimate goal. "I will build My church," Jesus had said, "and the gates of hell will not prevail against it." (See Matthew 16:18.)

No matter how "outnumbered" the Church of Jesus Christ might look, the ultimate victory belongs to God's saints. Don't be tempted to look at outward circumstances and give up; call upon God's innumerable angels to fight on your behalf. Then believe that you have their assistance, and step out in faith to fulfill God's call upon your life!

ANGELS AND THE RESURRECTED CHRIST

Angels were present throughout the life of Jesus as He walked this earth; they were present *before* He was born;

they were present *at His birth*; they were present *when He was an infant*; they were present *when He began His public ministry* and *when He neared the end of His ministry.* Do you think that the angels departed once Jesus laid down His life on the Cross? Never! It was an angel who rolled the stone away from His tomb:

> *And, behold, there was a great earthquake: for the angel of the Lord descended from heaven, and came and rolled back the stone from the door, and sat upon it* (Matthew 28:2).

How would you have liked to have had the assignment to roll the stone away from Jesus' tomb? Angels have the most thrilling chores! And when Mary came to the tomb, I think she saw two of the most special angels carrying out their special assignment:

> *But Mary stood without at the sepulchre weeping: and as she wept, she stooped down, and looked into the sepulchre, And seeth two angels in white sitting, the one at the head, and the other at the feet, where the body of Jesus had lain* (John 20:11,12).

I think that Mary saw the cherubim who overshadowed the Mercy Seat! Do you remember what God told Moses when He gave him instructions concerning the Mercy Seat? What Mary saw in the tomb of Jesus is clearly a picture of what God told Moses to build:

> *And thou shalt make a mercy seat of pure gold: two cubits and a half shall be the length thereof, and a cubit and a half the breadth thereof. And thou shalt make two cherubims of gold, of beaten work shalt thou make them, in the two ends of the mercy seat. And make one cherub on*

the one end, and the other cherub on the other end: even of the mercy seat shall ye make the cherubims on the two ends thereof (Exodus 25:17-19).

That's just what Mary saw: the two angels, or cherubim, one on each end of where the body of Jesus had lain. That means that JESUS is now the Mercy Seat! The angels were saying to Mary, "Jesus is the Mercy Seat, and He has risen from the dead!"

Jesus is YOUR Mercy Seat too. The angels on the top of the Ark of the Covenant had their eyes fixed upon the Mercy Seat where the shed blood was poured out. Now, whenever angels minister today to those of the household of faith, they always look to Jesus as the One Who shed His blood and as the One Who offers mercy and peace to anyone who calls out to Him.

ANGELS AT THE ASCENSION

We have seen that there were angels at every stage of Jesus' life: birth, childhood, ministry, death, and resurrection. There is only one event left to examine in the life of Jesus—His ascension. Are there any angels associated with His ascension? Yes! Two angels stood among the disciples as Jesus departed out of their view, and the angels had the most wonderful news:

And while they [the disciples] *looked stedfastly toward heaven as he went up, behold, two men stood by them in white apparel; Which also said, Ye men of Galilee, why stand ye gazing up into heaven? this same Jesus, which is taken up from you into heaven, shall so come in like manner as ye have seen him go into heaven* (Acts 1:10,11).

Just as angels were at the "head and feet" of where the body of Jesus lay, there were angels at the beginning and ending of Jesus' earthly life and ministry. Angels protected Him as an infant, ministered to Him when He began His public ministry, strengthened Him in His hour of pressure at Gethsemane, and rolled away the stone that covered His tomb.

God's angels are ready to go to work for you in the same way that they worked for Jesus. Don't overlook their powerful presence whenever you have a need that is in line with God's Word. Angels are all around you!

ANGELS AT THE SECOND COMING

We couldn't end this chapter without mentioning one more significant event associated with Jesus which includes the presence of angels—the Second Coming:

> *For the Son of man shall come in the glory of his Father with his angels; and then he shall reward every man according to his works* (Matthew 16:27).

> *For the Lord himself shall descend from heaven with a shout, with the voice of the archangel, and with the trump of God: and the dead in Christ shall rise first* (I Thessalonians 4:16).

Angels are waiting for that glorious day, and I pray that you are too! When I say that the angels are "waiting" for that day, I don't mean that they are sitting around with nothing to do in the meantime. Oh, no! After Jesus ascended, angels were kept *very* busy answering the prayers of the disciples in the early Church! And that's what we'll learn about in the next chapter.

Chapter Four

ANGELS AND THE DISCIPLES

Kidnapped! It's one word that will grip any mother's heart with fear, and it's the very word that raced through my mind many years ago when our six-year-old son's playmate told us, "Mike just took a ride in a yellow car."

A woman who was later diagnosed as a "psycho" was riding in a cab and stopped at the playground where Mike was having fun with a friend. She asked Mike to "go for a ride" with her; he got into the car alone, and off they went! I must tell you, when I heard what had happened, I was petrified! My husband Wally said to me, "Marilyn, we are going to pray; and God is going to return Mike safely within an hour."

We prayed; and God sent out angels to surround Mike, protect him, and bring him safely back. We also called the police; the police called the cab company; and *within an hour* the police caught the kidnapper in a park just as she was leaving the cab to enter another car.

Prayer activates angels! If you are not a praying Christian, you are a Christian who is open for the devil to wipe you out. And don't say you are too busy to pray! If you are too busy to pray, you are TOO BUSY!

ANGELS TO THE RESCUE!

The first-century Church was a praying Church—and many times we read how angels were sent to protect, instruct, and rescue the righteous. When 3,000 souls were added to the Church on the day of Pentecost and Peter healed a lame man at the Temple gate, the priests and the Sadducees became nervous:

> *And as they* [Peter and John] *spake unto the people, the priests, and the captain of the temple, and the Sadducees, came upon them, Being grieved that they taught the people, and preached through Jesus the resurrection from the dead* (Acts 4:1,2).

Peter and John were imprisoned overnight, warned not to preach about Jesus, and released. Did the threats silence the gospel? No. In fact, they had just the opposite effect:

> *And now, Lord, behold their threatenings: and grant unto thy servants, that with all boldness they may speak thy word* (Acts 4:29).

And speak they did! They not only *spoke* the Word, they *practiced* the Word:

> *There came also a multitude out of the cities round about unto Jerusalem, bringing sick folks, and them which were vexed with unclean spirits: and they were healed every one* (Acts 5:16).

That was too much for the high priest and the Sadducees! It was bad enough for the apostles to be preaching about the resurrection from the dead (something the Sadducees denied); but when multitudes were healed through the power of Jesus' name, these religious liberals were "filled with indignation"! (See Acts 5:17.) One translation of the Bible says they were filled with "jealousy." Where once the people looked to the Temple and its religious leaders for their spiritual and physical well-being, now the crowds had turned to some common fishermen who were spreading "lies" about a

Galilean named Jesus.

The way to stop all this preaching and healing, or so the high priest and Sadducees thought, was to put the apostles in prison once again. But that lasted only a short while:

> *And laid their hands on the apostles, and put them in the common prison. But the angel of the Lord by night opened the prison doors, and brought them forth, and said, Go, stand and speak in the temple to the people all the words of this life* (Acts 5:18-20).

Hallelujah! There hasn't been a prison built that can silence the Word of God.

I believe that angels delight in pulling God's children out of many types of "prisons." I remember reading the story of a Christian family which had visited a relative out in the country. In the back yard of the house was a deep pond. As the family prepared to leave, they heard screams from the back yard. Running to see what had happened, they discovered their four-year-old daughter standing sopping wet *several yards* from the pond!

There were no footprints leading from the pond to where their daughter was standing, and the only water outside the pond was in a puddle at the daughter's feet.

"Honey, what happened?" the mother asked.

The child was terribly frightened by the ordeal, but finally said that all she could remember was falling into the pond and "someone in white" pulling her out!

THE PRISONS WE MAKE

Another word for "prison" might be "bondage." Many times something in our lives can become a bondage or a prison for us. I know a woman whose tremendous guilt over mistakes she made while raising her children has become her prison. Despite the fact that her children have grown up and moved away, she still keeps thinking and asking herself (and others), "What did I do wrong?" "What could I have done differently?"

Sure, there are things we would do differently if we had the chance. But there comes a time when (if we have confessed our shortcomings to the Lord) we must say, "I did the best I could at the time. I made some mistakes. But God has forgiven me, and I am free from the past." Don't allow your past to become your prison. Allow God to deliver you from the guilt of past mistakes.

The apostle Paul at one time murdered some Christians and threw others into prison. There were many things in his past that Paul regretted, but he learned the secret to freeing himself from past sin and present guilt:

> *Brethren, I count not myself to have apprehended: but this one thing I do, forgetting those things which are behind, and reaching forth unto those things which are before, I press toward the mark for the prize of the high calling of God in Christ Jesus* (Philippians 3:13,14).

Hatred and bitterness can also become a prison. Have you ever known someone who was so obsessed with ill feelings toward an individual that it became a bondage? A businessman I'll call Harold was expecting a promotion. He'd been with the company for many years, was always on time, and always put in his full eight hours each day. When an opening occurred which he felt was just right for him, he told his wife to go shopping and buy a new dress. "I know that position is as good as mine, Sweetie," he told his wife.

Of course, Harold was devastated when the position went to a much younger associate. Bitterness began to grow within Harold, and before long all his conversations were peppered with digs against the officers of the company and the young associate. His attitude began to affect the quality of his work. His wife got tired of hearing him complain at home. Harold's bitterness became his bondage, and eventually he almost lost his job and his wife!

Through Christian counseling Harold learned to forgive those who had offended him and to release the situation at work to the Lord. He saw that trusting the Lord for promotions on the job freed him from a competitive spirit and allowed him to rejoice over *every* promotion within the office.

God wants ALL His children to be freed from the prisons of their own making. Angels can unlock *physical* prison doors; but only through your faith in God's Word, can God free you from the bondages of guilt and bitterness.

ACKNOWLEDGING ANGELIC ADVICE

Have you noticed that in the Bible *humans* always preach the gospel to other *humans*? Although there are perhaps millions of elect angels, and although God could send angels to share the gospel with people all over the earth, the Lord has seen fit to entrust the Great Commission to humans, not angels. But that doesn't mean that you and I can't get a little help from an angel now and then!

I have always enjoyed the story of Philip and the Ethiopian eunuch. Why? Because Philip was a *layman* in the early Church who was used by the Lord. Sometimes I think we get the idea that God only used the "big names" to do His work. When we think about the first-century Church, we might be tempted to think that it was the apostles who did all the work of preaching the gospel. Not so! In the gospels of Matthew, Mark, Luke, and John, we read about Philip the disciple. But in the book of Acts we read about another Philip—the *evangelist*. And this Philip did some evangelization with the help of an angel:

> *And the angel of the Lord spake unto Philip, saying, Arise, and go toward the south unto the way that goeth down from Jerusalem unto Gaza, which is desert* (Acts 8:26).

Philip was one of the seven men chosen to help in the distribution of food to the widows in the Church. He had the qualities needed to work closely with other people:

> *Wherefore, brethren, look ye out among you seven men of honest report, full of the Holy Ghost and wisdom, whom we may appoint over this business* (Acts 6:3).

Philip was honest, full of the Holy Spirit, and full of wisdom. God will use YOU in greater and greater ways as you cultivate those qualities. Now let's watch what Philip did in response to the angel's instructions:

> *And he arose and went:* . . . (Acts 8:27).

Because Philip was full of the Holy Spirit, he immediately obeyed the angel's words. How about you? Would you be willing to obey without question the words of an angel? Would you even recognize an angel if one appeared to you? Living in the Spirit will prepare you to have spiritual discernment and an obedient heart—which could make the difference between life and death for you or for someone else!

Many years ago I remember hearing the story of a Christian doctor who crawled out of bed on a snowy night because he heard someone knocking at his door. There stood the figure of a little girl who begged him to help her sick mother who lay ill several blocks away. The doctor quickly dressed and followed the little girl to her house.

The mother was indeed very ill and needed his expert attention. The doctor commented to the mother, "Your little girl must certainly be brave to have ventured out on a night like this. I don't know how she knew to knock at my door!"

"Doctor," the mother replied, "my daughter has been dead for some time now. Her little coat and hat are still hanging in the closet over there."

Sure enough, there in the closet was a *dry* coat and hat just like the ones worn by the little girl who had knocked on the doctor's door. Had God sent an angel in the form of a little girl to beckon that doctor? I don't know, but the doctor's obedience to the little girl's plea saved a life just as Philip's obedience to the angel brought salvation to the Ethiopian eunuch.

"Marilyn, I've never seen an angel; and I doubt that I ever will." I hear that comment whenever I teach on the subject of angels. What's my response? Just this: don't become centered upon "seeing angels," but center upon cultivating godly qualities like honesty; staying filled with the Holy Spirit; and being in the Word so that you'll have God's wisdom for every situation. Then, IF God chooses to send an angel to instruct you, you'll be ready to obey and carry out the angel's advice.

PETER AND CORNELIUS— THE ANGELIC "SETUP"

For over ten years following Pentecost, the Church was almost exclusively Jewish. And that was despite the fact that Israel's prophet Isaiah had clearly foretold of the gospel going to the gentiles:

> *And he said, It is a light thing that thou shouldest be my servant to raise up the tribes of Jacob, and to restore the preserved of Israel: I will also give thee for a light to the Gentiles, that thou mayest be my salvation unto the end of the earth* (Isaiah 49:6).
>
> *Thus saith the Lord GOD, Behold, I will lift up mine hand to the Gentiles, and set up my standard to the people: . . .* (Isaiah 49:22).
>
> *Arise, shine; for thy light is come, and the glory of the LORD is risen upon thee. And the Gentiles shall come to thy light, and kings to the brightness of thy rising* (Isaiah 60:1,3).
>
> *And I will set a sign among them, and I will send those that escape of them unto the nations, to Tarshish, Pul, and Lud, that draw the bow, to Tubal, and Javan, to the isles afar off, that have not heard my fame, neither have seen my glory; and they shall declare my glory among the Gentiles* (Isaiah 66:19).

For ten years the Church had ignored God's words through Isaiah and the words of Jesus in the Great Commission:

> *And Jesus came and spake unto them, saying, All power is given unto me in heaven and in*

earth. Go ye therefore, and teach all nations, baptizing them in the name of the Father, and of the Son, and of the Holy Ghost: (Matthew 28:18,19).

It finally took an angel to set up a meeting between Peter and a gentile named Cornelius:

There was a certain man in Caesarea called Cornelius, a centurion of the band called the Italian band, A devout man, and one that feared God with all his house, which gave much alms to the people, and prayed to God alway. He saw in a vision evidently about the ninth hour of the day an angel of God coming in to him, and saying unto him, Cornelius. And now send men to Joppa, and call for one Simon, whose surname is Peter (Acts 10:1-3,5).

Cornelius was quick to obey the angel. He sent two of his servants to Joppa where Peter was staying. I think it's interesting to see that the Lord sent an *angel* to Cornelius, but He paid a *personal* visit to Peter:

And there came a voice to him, Rise, Peter; kill and eat. But Peter said, Not so, Lord; for I have never eaten any thing that is common or unclean. And the voice spake unto him again the second time, What God hath cleansed, that call not thou common (Acts 10:13-15).

Peter had a strong Jewish background with an emphasis on separating himself from the heathen around him. But his upbringing obviously did not include taking God's message of hope and salvation to the gentiles! It took a visit from an angel and a visit from the Lord Himself to bring about a *gentile Pentecost.*

THE MESSENGER WHO HELPED SOLVE A MYSTERY

Angels are sometimes called ''messengers'' in the Bible. The *messenger* in the following story was not an angelic being sent directly from God; nevertheless, he delivered a message that brought about the answer to a family's prayer—and solved a 40-year mystery!

A family I'll call the Wilsons had five children. The oldest child, Tommy, was only six when the father died. Their mother was unable to care for the children and so they had to be adopted out among different families in their state of New York. All the children kept in touch through the years—all except Tommy. The family he had lived with moved out of state, and no one heard from him again.

Many years later as the children gathered for a reunion, someone suggested that everyone pray each day for one year for Tommy—if he was still alive—to somehow contact them. Nearly eleven months later Tommy did contact one of his brothers, and only then did the amazing details of his story become clear.

Tommy, at some point in his life, had received an injury that left him with amnesia. He couldn't remember anything that happened to him before the age of twenty. Other than the amnesia, he was quite happily engaged to be married (at age 46!) and planned a trip to his fiancee's hometown in New York.

When they were close to his fiancee's home, Tommy stopped at a small gas station and grocery store. When the cashier saw Tommy, he exclaimed, ''You sure look like Harry Wilson; you're not any relation to him, are you?''

As far as Tommy knew, his last name was Clarke; and

he didn't know of any "Harry." But the clerk was so struck by Tommy's likeness to Harry that he brought out a picture of the Wilson family he "happened to have" in the back room. "Now tell me you don't look just like one of them Wilsons," the clerk told Tommy.

Tommy and his fiancee decided to give the Wilsons a call—and you can guess the rest of the story! Tommy's brothers and sisters recognized him despite the number of years that had passed. Tommy slowly regained partial memory—all because his family had prayed and a gas station clerk had been used of the Lord to bring them together.

God is in the business of bringing families together—and believe me it takes less than amnesia to cause separation in families! Every day parents are fighting over custody of their children. In many instances children must be forcibly taken from abusive situations or from parents who are addicted to drugs or alcohol. Other families are torn apart through strife, bitterness, and jealousy.

Is *your* family whole, or are you longing for the day when every member will be present at the family reunion? Is there a son or daughter who has dropped out of sight as far as your family is concerned? Why not make a covenant with the Lord to pray each day for the next year for that family member to be reconciled. God is able to send His holy angels or human messengers along that person's path with just the right words to turn his or her heart toward home. The Lord used an angel to bring Peter and Cornelius together; He used a messenger to bring Tommy in contact with his family; and He can do the same to bring your family together again!

PETER, JAMES AND PRAYER

Does prayer *really* make a difference? Do angels *really* respond when Christians pray? To answer those questions I want to look with you at two appearances of angels in the twelfth chapter of Acts.

To understand the angelic actions in Acts 12 you need to understand the Herods. Let's begin with verse one of that chapter:

> *Now about that time Herod the king stretched forth his hands to vex certain of the church* (Acts 12:1).

There are a number of different "Herods" mentioned in the New Testament. Chapter two of Matthew refers to Herod the Great, who was an *Idumean.* That means that he was a descendant of the *Edomites.* Anyone who was a descendant of the Edomites was a descendant of Esau, the twin brother of Jacob.

When Jacob stole the family blessing from Esau, Esau vowed to kill him. We know that this conflict was later resolved, but the descendants of Esau hated the descendants of Jacob from that time on.

When the Israelites came out of Egypt and wanted to go through Edom—the country of the descendants of Esau—the Edomites refused to give them passage. The Edomites said, "No way! Your father Jacob deceived our father Esau, and we don't like you!"

That bitterness between the two tribes became a generational curse that passed right down to Herod the Great. At the time Jesus was born, the wise men came to Herod and told him about the new king and about the star that had led them to Jerusalem.

Herod the Great was not about to worship any other

king; he ordered the death of every male child under two years of age in the city of Bethlehem. Of course we've already seen how God sent an angel to Joseph to warn him of Herod's plan. Herod never did turn to God, and historians say he died a terrible, agonizing death.

Herod Antipas was the son of Herod the Great. He stole his brother's wife and refused to change his ways when John the Baptist confronted him publicly regarding his sin. Herod had John thrown into prison where John still witnessed to Herod. Unfortunately for John, Herod offered to give his wife's daughter anything she wanted (up to half of his kingdom!) because her sensual dancing took away his sense! At the coaxing of her mother, she asked for John's head on a platter.

Herod Agrippa I is the Herod mentioned in Acts 12. He was the grandson of Herod the Great which, of course, makes him an Idumean or an Edomite—a descendant of Esau. The Herods were always mean and vicious against God's people, and this Herod ordered the first execution of an apostle:

> *And he killed James the brother of John with the sword* (Acts 12:2).

Then he decided, "Oh, boy, the Jews liked that; it gave me real favor with them. I think I'll have Peter killed; he's one of their leaders too":

> *And because he saw it pleased the Jews, he proceeded further to take Peter also. (Then were the days of unleavened bread.) And when he had apprehended him, he put him in prison, and delivered him to four quaternions of soldiers to keep him; intending after Easter to bring him forth to the people* (Acts 12:3,4).

Peter was chained to two guards and watched by two other guards. Every three hours another group of four soldiers would come in and relieve the prior guards. It was obvious that Peter was an important prisoner, and it certainly looked as if there was "no way out" for him.

The Bible doesn't say that prayer was made for James; but the Church wised up really fast when Peter was put in prison:

> *Peter therefore was kept in prison: but prayer was made without ceasing of the church unto God for him* (Acts 12:5).

I think when James was killed the devil got a jump on God's people. I think that Herod probably just grabbed him up and killed him right away. The Church was stunned and not experienced in this kind of thing yet. But when Peter was arrested, the Church said, "Hey, we can't let the devil just walk away with everything." So they began to pray—and God answered by sending an angel to rescue Peter.

Praying God's Word is the way to activate angels. Don't sit around whining and crying that you never see the supernatural. Get into the Word, pray the Word, and exercise faith in the Word!

Now look at how God used an angel to answer the prayers of the Church:

> *And, behold, the angel of the Lord came upon him, and a light shined in the prison: and he smote Peter on the side, and raised him up, saying, Arise up quickly. And his chains fell off from his hands. And the angel said unto him, Gird thyself, and bind on thy sandals. And so he did. And he saith unto him, Cast thy garment*

about thee, and follow me. And he went out, and followed him; and wist not that it was true which was done by the angel; but thought he saw a vision (Acts 12:7-9).

Peter did not believe his eyes! He thought he was dreaming. But this was no dream:

When they were past the first and the second ward, they came unto the iron gate that leadeth unto the city; which opened to them of his own accord: and they went out, and passed on through one street; and forthwith the angel departed from him (Acts 12:10).

Notice that the angel left Peter when his work was done. Angels aren't sent to satisfy our curiosity or to chat. They are sent to do a job; and when their assignment is finished, they return to the Father to await another task.

Peter didn't wait around either; he went to where the Church was praying without ceasing. Peter knocked, but the maid who answered the door excitedly ran off to tell the others without unlocking the door!

The Jews believed in guardian angels; and when they heard the servant girl claim that Peter was at the front door, they assumed it was his angel:

And they said unto her, Thou art mad. But she constantly affirmed that it was even so. Then said they, It is his angel (Acts 12:15).

But Peter was no angel! He related to them all how God had rescued him with the help of an angel. Then he departed to someplace where Herod wouldn't find him.

HEROD AND THE ANGEL OF JUDGMENT

For believers, angels are sent by God to bless, to protect,

and to rescue. For those who are against God's people, angels bring judgment. Such was the case for Herod. God could have struck Herod dead after he killed James. But in the Lord's mercy, Herod was allowed to live despite his hatred for the Christians. However, Herod allowed his subjects to worship him in place of God; and the Lord said, "That's it!":

> *And the people gave a shout, saying, It is the voice of a god, and not of a man. And immediately the angel of the Lord smote him, because he gave not God the glory: and he was eaten of worms, and gave up the ghost* (Acts 12:22,23).

What a contrast! The Herods were constantly confronted with the claims of God by John the Baptist, the Magi, and the apostles. But their hearts were hard as stone. They sought only to wipe out their opposition, but God used angels to outsmart them every step of the way. Eventually God used an angel to stop the line of Herods from carrying their bitterness any further. After the book of Acts, we never hear of the Herods—or Idumeans—again!

There is one last account in the book of Acts of an angel appearing. This time the angel traveled with Paul on his voyage to Rome to face trial before Caesar Nero:

> *Then Festus, when he had conferred with the council, answered, Hast thou* [Paul] *appealed unto Caesar? unto Caesar shalt thou go* (Acts 25:12).

On the voyage a storm arose, and it wasn't until all those aboard the ship had given up hope for survival that an angel appeared to Paul to bring encouragement and comfort:

And when neither sun nor stars in many days appeared, and no small tempest lay on us, all hope that we should be saved was then taken away. But after long abstinence Paul stood forth in the midst of them, and said, . . . I exhort you to be of good cheer: for there shall be no loss of any man's life among you, but of the ship. For there stood by me this night the angel of God, whose I am, and whom I serve (Acts 27:20-23).

Do you remember the angel who spoke to the shepherds at the time of Jesus' birth? His message was "Fear not." Paul's angel (Could it have been the same angel? I don't know.) proclaimed the same message:

. . . Fear not, Paul; thou must be brought before Caesar; and, lo, God hath given thee all them that sail with thee (Acts 27:24).

True to the angel's word, Paul and all the ship's passengers escaped from the ship to land. Did God send an angel to help Paul because Paul was some "big name" in the Church? Certainly not! God is no respecter of persons, and there is only ONE big name in the Church—JESUS. What the Lord did for Peter and Paul, He will do for YOU as you pray without ceasing, pray the Word, and exercise faith in the Word. God's angels are sent out to minister to the household of faith—that's *you*. And as we'll see in the next chapter, God's angels are very active in the *present* to keep you from making a shipwreck of your faith!

Chapter Five

ANGELS IN THE PRESENT

Have you ever wondered if you REALLY see your whole life in front of you just before you die? I had a near-death encounter once that made me think, "This is it!" I didn't see my whole life in front of me, but I did think my life had come to an end!

I was in St. Louis at one of my Bible Encounters where I teach through the entire Bible in 21 hours. After the second evening of teaching, I was a passenger with a friend who was driving me back to the hotel where I was staying. There had been an accident on the left-hand side of the road; and all at once, a car pulled out of the oncoming lane. It was heading straight for us—and fast! My friend swerved a little bit, but we couldn't pull out of the way into the other lane because of the other traffic.

I honestly don't know where the other car went, but it didn't hit us. I thought, "God, is this a dream? Am I awake? Is this really real?"

It wasn't a dream, and I believe that angels saved our lives that night. Every morning I pray that angels will go before and behind me to protect me. I ask the Father to make my way straight and to keep me in all my ways.

My friend said, "Thank God! Every time I get into this car, I ask angels to go before and behind it."

Now you may say this was just happenstance, but I don't believe that. There are no happenstances with God. And that's why you and I need the ministry of angels in the present—to minister to those of us in the household of faith:

But to which of the angels said he at any time, Sit on my right hand, until I make thine enemies thy footstool? Are they not all ministering spirits, sent forth to minister for them who shall be heirs of salvation? (Hebrews 1:13,14).

HAGAR AND THE MINISTRY OF ANGELS

Would it surprise you to learn that Hagar was a member of the household of faith who experienced the ministry of angels? Hagar was a young Egyptian slave girl who had accompanied Abraham (Abram) and Sarah (Sarai) when they left Egypt. There had been a famine in the Promised Land, and Abraham had disobeyed God by fleeing to Egypt to escape the famine. Once there, Abraham lied about Sarah being his wife and ended up in all kinds of trouble. It's never wise to use your human reasoning. Abraham thought it would be better to disobey God and to live in Egypt rather than to trust the Lord to meet his needs. As a result, Sarah picked up some customs that she shouldn't have touched with a ten-foot pole!

God had promised Abraham a son, but Sarah found herself childless month after month. Finally she resorted to the heathen custom of allowing her husband to have a child by one of his slave girls. There are some things we learn from the unsaved that we need to forget! The ways of the world are never going to be a blessing to the Christian.

Abraham went along with Sarah's scheme, but Sarah wasn't too happy when Hagar stopped much of her work after she was a few months pregnant. Plus, I think Sarah was jealous of Hagar. Any woman watching her husband's baby growing inside someone else would be jealous. Sarah finally had enough mental torture, and she drove Hagar away.

Where could Hagar go but back to Egypt? She was a young girl in a hopeless situation, but she knew how to pray. She had been a part of Abraham's household, and Abraham's house knew the Lord:

> *And the LORD said, Shall I hide from Abraham that thing which I do; For I know him, that he will command his children and his household after him, and they shall keep the way of the LORD, to do justice and judgment; that the LORD may bring upon Abraham that which he hath spoken of him* (Genesis 18:17,19).

Hagar was fortunate to be part of Abraham's household. The blessing of Abraham affected even the lowliest slave girl. Hagar knew about the God of Abraham so she prayed, and God heard her prayers by sending an angel:

> *And the angel of the LORD found her by a fountain of water in the wilderness, by the fountain in the way to Shur* (Genesis 16:7).

God knew all about Hagar's situation, yet the angel asked her to explain her situation:

> *And he said, Hagar, Sarai's maid, whence camest thou? and whither wilt thou go? And she said, I flee from the face of my mistress Sarai* (Genesis 16:8).

Sometimes when we're faced with a crisis, it's good to remember where we've come from. It's all too easy to forget what the Lord has done for us in the past. I have known of dear Christians who have seen God work miracles on their behalf to get them to the mission field. But when they faced their first real test of faith, they forgot about what had happened in the past, called it quits, and left the mission field in despair. They failed to remember God's past faithfulness.

The angel also asked Hagar where she planned to go. That's a good question for us too. Where will we go if we backslide and call it quits concerning our faith? Anyone who has truly been born again will be miserable if he or she goes back to the old way of living. When the rough times come, Christians should rehearse past victories and trust God for the future.

The angel told Hagar to return to Sarah and submit to her. That would have been difficult! Along with that command, the angel gave Hagar some promises concerning her son:

> *And the angel of the LORD said unto her, I will multiply thy seed exceedingly, that it shall not be numbered for multitude. And the angel of the LORD said unto her, Behold, thou art with child, and shalt bear a son, and shalt call his name Ishmael; because the LORD hath heard thy affliction. And he will be a wild man; his hand will be against every man, and every man's hand against him; and he shall dwell in the presence of all his brethren* (Genesis 16:10-12).

This young girl's life was touched by all this attention. Why had God sent His angel to minister to Hagar? Because she was of the household of faith! Hagar was sitting by a well when the angel found her, and the well was called *Beer-lahai-roi,* meaning "The living God seest me." Hagar was saying, "God not only heard my prayers but He also saw my need.'' The Lord always hears the prayers and sees the needs of those who are of the household of faith.

ISHMAEL AND GOD'S ANGEL

Hagar's troubles didn't end when she went back and put herself under Sarah's authority. I don't think Sarah ever got over being jealous of Hagar and Ishmael. On the day when Isaac was weaned, Ishmael was teasing him; and Sarah didn't like it:

> *And Sarah saw the son of Hagar the Egyptian, which she had born unto Abraham, mocking. Wherefore she said unto Abraham, Cast out this bondwoman and her son: for the son of this bondwoman shall not be heir with my son, even with Isaac* (Genesis 21:9,10).

Sarah hadn't changed a bit; she drove Hagar out when she was pregnant; and now Sarah wanted Hagar *and* Ishmael kicked out. Of course that attitude grieved Abraham; he loved Ishmael as any father would love his firstborn. But God must have known the conflict in Abraham's heart over his two sons and over which one was to inherit the family blessing. ''Do what Sarah has asked you,'' God told Abraham. ''And don't worry about Ishmael. I'm going to make a nation from his seed too.''

Abraham believed God and sent Hagar and Ishmael (now a teenager) off into the desert with only some bread and a bottle of water:

> *And Abraham rose up early in the morning, and took bread, and a bottle of water, and gave it unto Hagar, putting it on her shoulder, and the child, and sent her away: and she departed,*

and wandered in the wilderness of Beer-sheba (Genesis 21:14).

Poor Hagar; she was wandering once again! Once the water ran out, Hagar knew that death was not far away. She couldn't bear to see her only child die, so she left him under a shrub and sat off in the distance out of eyesight. The Bible says she wept. Only a mother can feel her anguish and share her sorrow!

The situation looked hopeless once again, but Ishmael had grown up in Abraham's household. This meant that Ishmael knew the God of Abraham! So Ishmael prayed, God heard, and once again an angel was assigned to minister to those in the household of faith:

And God heard the voice of the lad; and the angel of God called to Hagar out of heaven, and said unto her, What aileth thee, Hagar? fear not; for God hath heard the voice of the lad where he is (Genesis 21:17).

One of the most important things Christians need to teach their children is how to pray. You may say, "Oh, but I pray for my children." That's wonderful; I pray for my children too. But the greatest thing you can do for them is to teach them to pray for themselves. Let them develop a prayer life on their own. That's what Abraham did with Ishmael—taught him how to pray. Ishmael didn't have just *instruction* in prayer; he no doubt had his father's *example* of prayer also.

The angel assigned to Hagar and Ishmael liked to ask questions. "What's the problem, Hagar? Don't be afraid!" God had heard the prayers of Ishmael; and He was not only going to spare Ishmael's life but God was also going to make a great nation from his seed.

Sometimes we forget God's promise or covenant to Hagar concerning Ishmael. We think about God's covenant with Abraham and Isaac, and we think that God is only concerned with the "big names."

You might be tempted to think, "God's not going to assign an angel to me; I'm not Billy Graham." That's right; you're *not* Billy Graham. But Billy Graham is not *the* big name. Who is the big name? Jesus! And does everyone who is born again have access to that name? Yes. Does God want to send angels to the entire household of faith or just to those who are well-known? The Lord is concerned with each and every person who names the name of Jesus!

One reason we might not experience angelic ministry is because we get our eyes on people and become offended by what they do. Ishmael could have said, "My own father has rejected me." Hagar could have shaken her fist at heaven and said, "God, where are You that You would have let Abraham and Sarah do this to me?" Both Ishmael and Hagar could have become bitter and revengeful. Do you think they would have received angelic ministry if they had hardened their hearts to the things of God? No way!

Do *you* want the ministry of angels in your situation? Let me ask you. Are you speaking doubts, fears, and anger? Are you whining, gossiping, and full of strife and confusion? Sometimes we have such ugly attitudes that angels probably don't want to be around us! Hagar and Ishmael kept their attitudes right, looked to God's provisions, and angels ministered to their needs.

JOHN, THE TRACTOR, AND GOD'S ANGELS

John had been a farmer for over 60 years and a member of the household of faith for nearly 40 years. His favorite verse had always been, "Ask and you shall receive." When the grass on his farm needed cutting, John hitched a set of mower blades to his tractor and set off to level the grass.

When he had finished, John stopped the tractor on a slight uphill grade and got out to unhitch the blades. Suddenly he was pinned by the tractor as it rolled backward, taking away his breath and leaving him at the point of unconsciousness. That's when he *asked*, "Dear Lord, please move this tractor so I can get free!"

In answer to his prayer, the tractor moved *uphill* just enough to free John. "Twelve men couldn't have pushed that tractor uphill like that," John says. But John is a member of the household of faith; and I believe John received an angelic visitation that saved his life. God heard and saw his plight just as God had seen the plight of Hagar and Ishmael. The Lord's angels are waiting for His command in order to rush to the aid of Christians.

Is the Lord hearing you pray or complain? Does the Lord see your situation or does He see that your attitude needs to be changed? Don't forget, God's angels minister to the household of *faith*!

DEMONIC ACTIVITY

While two-thirds of the original angels minister to God's family, we must not forget that one-third of the angels are under the leadership of Satan with the express purpose of tempting, harassing, and bringing believers *and* unbelievers into failure and defeat.

When my husband and I were very new in full-time ministry for the Lord, a woman picked our name out of the telephone directory. She called and said that she was having a nervous breakdown. It never occurred to us that the woman might be under the influence of a demon, so we drove to her house to pray for her.

When we entered the house, we saw a pretty woman about 27 years old. She was rocking back and forth—something we thought was caused by nervousness. We tried to talk with her, but she was incoherent. My husband Wally knelt down by the couch where she was rocking and said, "I rebuke you, Satan, in Jesus' name!"

When Wally said that, the most chilling thing happened: she started talking in another voice that said, "I'll come out of her and into *you*!"

If there had been room to jump under that couch, I would have done it! I was terribly frightened; that was my very first encounter with a demon-possessed person. Wally started praying and speaking against the devil in the name of Jesus. Then he remembered the time when the disciples asked Jesus why they had failed to cast a demon out of a boy. Jesus told them that some demons do not come out but by prayer and fasting (see Matthew 17:21).

We left her house, and she was taken to a mental hospital. Our church began to fast. Some fasted one meal a day, while my husband went on a full fast for seven days. I went to the hospital every day and read the Word to her.

Eventually she was given a pass and came to our church. Seven or eight of us began to pray for her. I won't say that we did everything right, but our hearts were sincere. God showed us that demon spirits had come into that woman when she was in high school. She had been involved in sexual impurity, and she had a very vile mouth. That lifestyle continued for years, and now the demons were really tormenting her to the point of a nervous breakdown.

We had her repent of her past impurity and her foul mouth. She turned to the Lord in earnest and was set free! She experienced the truth found in the twelfth chapter of Revelation:

> *And they overcame him* [the devil] *by the blood of the Lamb, and by the word of their testimony; and they loved not their lives unto the death* (Revelation 12:11).

PAUL AND DEMONS

We've already seen how an angel saved Paul and the entire crew of a ship headed for Rome. Paul belonged to the household of faith; that meant he could expect the ministry of angels. But it also meant that he could expect the opposition of fallen angels. Notice I said "expect" and *not* "fear." Believers have authority over demons, but Christians must first discern demonic activity before they can take action–just as Paul did while traveling through Philippi.

The devil is very devious and crafty; everyone who "talks" religion is not spiritual. While Paul was preaching the gospel in Philippi, a woman followed him, calling out a very "religious" sounding message:

> *And it came to pass, as we went to prayer, a certain damsel possessed with a spirit of divination met us, which brought her master*

> *much gain by soothsaying: The same followed Paul and us, and cried, saying, These men are the servants of the most high God, which shew unto us the way of salvation* (Acts 16:16,17).

The evil spirit was saying all the right things. This girl's owners, however, used her to make money by telling fortunes. Many Christians today are involved in "innocent" fortunetelling like reading the horoscope in the newspaper, reading tea leaves, playing with Ouija boards, and similar "games." If you are dabbling in any of these things, get out! Sometimes the oppression we feel as believers has come from something back in our childhoods that we thought was innocent fun. These things are dangerous, and Christians need to exercise discernment in this area to eliminate the evil spirits behind occult practices.

Notice that Paul spoke to the spirit, not to the girl:

> *And this did she many days. But Paul, being grieved, turned and said to the spirit, I command thee in the name of Jesus Christ to come out of her. And he came out the same hour* (Acts 16:18).

Paul was not against the woman; he was against the spirit that had possessed her body. The evil spirit didn't come out immediately, but within the hour that girl was set free. I have prayed with people who were demon possessed, and I didn't see any immediate results. But by the next morning, they were free and had started walking in liberty and freedom!

Make no mistake about it; sin opens the door to demonic influence. Another woman in the Bible who was possessed by demons was Mary Magdalene:

And certain women, which had been healed of evil spirits and infirmities, Mary called Magdalene, out of whom went seven devils (Luke 8:2).

The Bible doesn't say whether this Mary was a prostitute, but that is just the kind of sexual activity that opens the door for demon possession. Sexual uncleanness will get you into all kinds of trouble. That doesn't mean you should be in fear if you've committed sexual sins; Jesus came to set the captives free!

FALLEN ANGELS AND THE SON OF GOD

Would you like to know one thing that really upsets me? It upsets me to know that demons are smarter than some people! I've talked to atheists who have argued that there couldn't be a God. That just doesn't make sense to me when even the devil knows that there is a God:

Thou believest that there is one God; thou doest well: the devils also believe, and tremble (James 2:19).

Demons have more intelligence than some people! When Jesus was walking this earth, the demons knew Who He was and what He had come to do:

And when he was come to the other side into the country of the Gergesenes, there met him two possessed with devils, coming out of the tombs, exceeding fierce, so that no man might pass by that way. And, behold, they cried out, saying, What have we to do with thee, Jesus, thou Son of God? art thou come hither to torment us before the time? (Matthew 8:28,29).

The devils knew *two* things that atheists and modernists in the Church don't know: Jesus is the Son of God, and hell was created for the devil and his angels. The devil and his demons know what the future holds for them, and they are trying to take as many people with them as possible! And if they can't take you with them, the devil will harass you and tempt you to neutralize your effectiveness as a Christian. But God has given us the *one* weapon that works against the devil: His Word.

When Satan tempted Jesus in the wilderness (see Matthew 4), he quoted from the Bible! Only the devil twisted the Scripture a bit to suit his own purpose. He did the same thing when he tempted Eve in the Garden of Eden.

If you don't know your Bible, I mean REALLY know your Bible, you don't have one thing to overcome the devil. You may be a born-again believer, but the devil will take the meat out of your sandwich, rain on your picnic, and beat you up spiritually if you don't take the offensive against him with the Word of God.

When the devil came to Jesus and quoted from the Old Testament, Jesus countered him with "It is written . . . ," "It is written . . . ." If you don't know what is "written," then you don't stand a chance when the devil whispers in your ear and twists the Bible around to suit his own lying plans. If you are a Christian, you are in a battle with a host of fallen angels. Your weapon is the Word of God. If you haven't picked it up for weeks, months, or years, go find it and start reading it every day!

DEMONS AND DOCTRINES

Once we know the Word, we'll be safe from false doctrines that are actually spread through the Church by demons:

> *Now the Spirit speaketh expressly, that in the latter times some shall depart from the faith, giving heed to seducing spirits, and doctrines of devils* (I Timothy 4:1).

There are some demon spirits who try to seduce Christians away from God's Word through doctrines that are divisive and downright false. These doctrines may sound sweet and religious, but they are not found in the Bible. If you don't know the Bible, you will be fooled into following their teaching. What should you do? Follow the words of the apostle John:

> *Beloved, believe not every spirit, but try the spirits whether they are of God: because many false prophets are gone out into the world* (I John 4:11).

What does it mean to "try the spirits"? It means to be a fruit inspector! Jesus said that we would know true disciples by their fruit. Are they committed to the local church? Are they really committed to the Word alone? Does strife follow them? If they are causing division, avoid them like the plague! The Word is to edify us, to build us up. If someone comes to your door with a funny sounding doctrine, check it out with the Word. It may be a doctrine of devils. If it is, tell him, "It is written . . . ," "It is written . . . ."

ANGELS: MINISTRY OR MENACE?

Christians are in the middle of a great angelic conflict. Fortunately, we are on the winning side! God has provided His angels to minister to the household of faith while the devil and his angels try to harass, tempt, and cause Christians to stumble in their faith. The key to angelic *ministry* or angelic *menace* for the Christian in this war is knowing the Word of God. The Word of God has at least ten pieces of strategic advice to offer Christians:

1. Put on the whole armor of God:
   Put on the whole armour of God, that ye may be able to stand against the wiles of the devil (Ephesians 6:11).
2. Know Satan's devices:
   Lest Satan should get an advantage of us: for we are not ignorant of his devices (II Corinthians 2:11).
3. Give the devil no place:
   Neither give place to the devil (Ephesians 4:27).
4. Resist the devil:
   Submit yourselves therefore to God. Resist the devil, and he will flee from you (James 4:7).
5. Be sober and vigilant:
   Be sober, be vigilant; because your adversary the devil, as a roaring lion, walketh about, seeking whom he may devour (I Peter 5:8).
6. Overcome the devil by the blood:
   And they overcame him by the blood of the lamb, and by the word of their testimony; and they loved not their lives unto the death (Revelation 12:11)
7. Overcome the devil by the Word:

I have written unto you, fathers, because ye have known him that is from the beginning. I have written unto you, young men, because ye are strong, and the word of God abideth in you, and ye have overcome the wicked one (I John 2:14).

8. Cast out devils in the name of Jesus:
And these signs shall follow them that believe; In my name shall they cast out devils; they shall speak with new tongues (Mark 16:17).
9. Overcome the devil by the power of the Holy Spirit:
For as many as are led by the Spirit of God, they are the sons of God. For ye have not received the spirit of bondage again to fear; but ye have received the Spirit of adoption, whereby we cry, Abba, Father (Romans 8:14,15).
10. Overcome the devil by faith:
For whatsoever is born of God overcometh the world: and this is the victory that overcometh the world, even our faith (I John 5:4).

Which will it be? Ministry or menace? The choice is up to *you*. God has provided everything needed for Christians to receive angelic ministry in this present age and to overcome demonic menacing.

In the next chapter, I want to look with you at a tactic that Satan uses to subtly drag Christians down and render them ineffective in God's kingdom: depression. God's Word has the answers to this deadly "wile" of the devil!

Chapter Six

ANGELS, DEPRESSION, AND YOU

Many years ago I went through an experience in which I felt depression rising up to overwhelm me. It was the evening of the 21st of December, 1976. I had planned a family evening consisting of a good dinner, a game, and an early bedtime. Our family loves artichokes, and the grocery had had some lovely fresh ones. I had bought four of them for our dinner, Swiss steak was in the oven, and I was mixing the dressing for our salad when the phone rang.

My mother's voice was soft and difficult to hear. I asked her to speak louder; and when she tried, she broke into sobs. An ambulance had taken my father to Denver General Hospital because of a surprise heart attack. I quickly washed my hands and called to my husband, who was reading the evening newspaper.

I turned off the oven and the front burner where the artichokes were steaming. My son and daughter were called into the front room where we prayed. I hurriedly brushed my hair and put on the warmest coat I had. Driving to the hospital, I rebuked the fear and depression rising in my heart. I parked near the emergency room and hurried through the parking lot with icy winds darting around my ankles. My mother and two of her friends were sitting in the waiting room. She was white and drawn as we joined hands and I prayed for her.

Soon the doctor joined us, assuring us that everything possible was being done. After an hour, they moved my father to intensive care on the third floor. The four of us followed him on the elevator. It seemed that we waited for hours, but it was only about 45 minutes. When the doctor entered the waiting room, we knew the news by the expression on his face. My father was dead!

My mother broke out in loud, convulsive sobs as we gathered around her to comfort her. I remembered how warm and open my father had been the last six months. Sometimes my mother and I had questioned his behavior. Was he *really* born again? But the last six months had been different. My father had actually witnessed to a Moslem working in the neighborhood grocery store. One Sunday the man had accompanied my father to my Sunday school class where we were studying the blood covenant. My father had been studying the Bible with us even outside church. Yes, the last six months, without a doubt, showed the evidence of his conversion. Yet I still had to fight back a wave of depression that tried to engulf me.

I took my mother to her modest home in west Denver. I wanted her to spend the night with us; but she insisted, saying that she could only sleep in her own bed. It was after 11:00 p.m. when I finally arrived home. I had already called from the hospital and told my family of my father's death.

I unlocked the front door as quietly as possible, not wanting to awaken the children. My husband fixed me a cup of coffee, and we sat and talked for an hour. As I prepared for bed, I prayed for my mother that she might rest well. It happened so quickly—was my father's death really true? It seemed like a bad dream.

The firm, hard bed felt so good! I slid between the sheets knowing that I could sleep because of the peace that only Jesus gives. Suddenly, I awakened, looked at our digital clock, and saw that it was 2:30 in the morning. Then thoughts about my father began to race through my head. He was dead, and it wasn't a dream. The grief of his death hit me as a hard, cold reality. How could I cope with my feelings?

I started to awaken my husband so that he could pray for me, but then I remembered that Sunday services would begin in a few hours and that he would need his strength for the added responsibilities in the days ahead. I chose not to disturb him. Instead I lay quietly.

It was then a light and a warmth came into the room. With fascination I watched as it moved toward me. I felt the touch of the light and warmth as it permeated my own chest. Instantly my grief disappeared, and I realized that my guardian angel had touched me. I knew then, as never before, that not only had Jesus carried my sins, but He had also carried my griefs and sorrows. I fell asleep again, but this time it was in peace and with an indescribable joy. Once more that night I felt the same angelic touch.

My father's funeral was in no way the depressing ceremony that funerals often are. Our administrative pastor of Happy Church ministered. The funeral was held the 23rd of December. The text was, "I, John, saw the new Jerusalem." My father's name was John. He was not *hearing* of the new Jerusalem; he was standing on the streets of the new Jerusalem and enjoying all its wonders—including the very presence of the Lamb of God!

Later, I asked the Lord, "Why did I have such an unusual experience the night of my father's death?" His answer came in the early part of January as I was seated in an airplane on my way to a leadership conference in Hawaii. As I sat on the long flight, I looked out the window at the green waves edged in silver below. It was a quiet time of meditation. I thought of the night of the angelic visitation, and with curiosity I again questioned the Lord about the angelic visitation. Quickly, the Lord gave me an answer—not in an audible voice, but through my thought life. This is perfectly natural for a Christian because Paul wrote in I Corinthians 2:16 that we have the mind of Christ. And this was the Lord's revelation to me: "I allowed you to have a small taste of the glory which your father entered into."

God had helped me overcome depression, grief, and fear through the ministry of His angel. The Lord can do the same for you!

To show you how *good* the Lord is, the following year on the night of the anniversary of my father's death, I was again awakened at 2:30 in the morning. The same warmth and light came into our bedroom and permeated my spirit. My guardian angel had been sent by my heavenly Father with some extra comfort on that particular night of sentiment and sorrow. Praise the Lord!

ANGELS, DEPRESSION, AND GIDEON

Are angels just for "special people"? Do you think that angels minister to *other* people but that they somehow pass you by? Angels aren't reserved for the mighty in faith or for those who are "holy" and "righteous." Angels are for anyone in need! One such person was Gideon, and his circumstances should encourage you whenever you're feeling "down" on yourself!

The Biblical account of Gideon is found in Judges 6-8. Israel was in serious trouble with a large tribe of nomads called the Midianites. The Israelites had deserted God's laws and commandments. Because of their sin, the Israelites were paying heavily. The Midianites had oppressed them for seven years—furiously riding through the Hebrew villages, burning the Israelites' crops, and crushing their hopes of peace.

The oppression of the Midianites became so fierce and cruel that the Hebrews were forced to live in caves in the high rocky hills. Some dug underground hiding places for their food and families. Because of the cowardice of the Hebrews, others such as the Amalekites joined in the foraging. In the harvesttimes, the Midianites, Amalekites, and related tribes would come in such vast numbers that the Bible likens them to grasshoppers. Their purpose was not only to steal but they also wanted to destroy the land. The Hebrews were without sheep, goats, and oxen for they had long since been stolen by the Midianites.

Imagine the depression that set in among the Israelites! The situation looked absolutely hopeless. Finally the Hebrews came to the place where they could no longer cope, and they did what *you and I* should do when we find ourselves in the depths of despair: they cried out to the Lord.

The Lord responded to their cries by sending a prophet with a message of repentance:

> *And it came to pass, when the children of Israel cried unto the LORD because of the Midianites, That the LORD sent a prophet unto the children of Israel, which said unto them, Thus saith the LORD God of Israel, I brought you up from Egypt, and brought you forth out of the house of bondage; And I delivered you out of the hand of the Egyptians, and out of the hand of all that*

> *oppressed you, and drave them out from before you, and gave you their land; And I said unto you, I am the LORD your God; fear not the gods of the Amorites, in whose land ye dwell: but ye have not obeyed my voice* (Judges 6:7-10).

What's the first step in overcoming depression? Repent! Depression is a sin; yes, a sin. When we're depressed, what we're really saying is that God is no longer in control of our lives or of the events that impact our lives. Depression is the road to atheism. It's saying in our hearts, "There is no God."

Notice the antidote for depression that the prophet administered; he said in so many words, "Remember God's reality in your past." For the Israelites, the Lord's reality was seen in the way they were delivered from Egypt, delivered from the Egyptians, brought into the Promised Land, and their triumph over all their enemies in the new land. If looking at the *future* makes you depressed, then look at God's goodness in the *past*, and you'll find your faith restored.

Repentance brings in the presence of the Lord. After Israel repented, the Lord sent an angel to change their hopeless situation:

> *And there came an angel of the LORD, and sat under an oak which was in Ophrah, that pertained unto Joash the Abi-ezrite: and his son Gideon threshed wheat by the winepress, to hide it from the Midianites* (Judges 6:11).

Normally we think that God sends His angels to those who are "spiritual." Isn't that right? Haven't you thought, "I'll never get any help from an angel; that's for other people." Wrong! Angels are for everyone in the household of faith, and that means *you* if you're a Christian.

Gideon was the least likely candidate for an angelic visit—if we were to judge on the basis of ''spirituality.'' Every time Gideon opened his mouth, out popped such words of inferiority that it was obvious to see why Gideon had an angel assigned to him—this guy needed help!

The name *Gideon* means ''warrior.'' When we first read about Gideon, he was not living up to his name. He was hiding from the Midianites and secretly threshing barley. It must have been very shocking for Gideon to look up and see an angel sitting under an oak tree. Angels always appear so calm, and isn't that just what we need when we're depressed and worried? The angel's words to Gideon were powerful truths:

> *And the angel of the LORD appeared unto him, and said unto him, The LORD is with thee, thou mighty man of valour* (Judges 6:12).

Angels look at those they minister to through the eyes of God's Word. In other words, angels see us with a *faith look*. Gideon was anything but a ''mighty man of valor.'' His reply to the angel shows us just how depressed and unbelieving he was:

> *And Gideon said unto him, Oh my Lord, if the LORD be with us, why then is all this befallen us? and where be all his miracles which our fathers told us of, saying, Did not the LORD bring us up from Egypt? but now the LORD hath forsaken us, and delivered us into the hands of the Midianites* (Judges 6:13).

When we're depressed, our reasoning goes out the window! God had not delivered the Israelites into the hands of the Midianites; the Israelites, by their own disobedience to God's Word, had delivered themselves into the hands of the Midianites. When we disobey the Lord, we leave a hole in the hedge of our protection; the devil then has access to us.

Fortunately for all of Israel, the angel ignored Gideon's depressed state of being and continued to speak faith-filled words to him:

> *And the LORD looked upon him, and said, Go in this thy might, and thou shalt save Israel from the hand of the Midianites: have not I sent thee?* (Judges 6:14).

With such powerful words from an angel, you would think that Gideon would be lifted from his morass of despondency—but not so! Sometimes when we're down on ourselves, it takes a while to come to our senses. Gideon had the nerve to argue with the angel:

> *And he said unto him, Oh my Lord, wherewith shall I save Israel? behold, my family is poor in Manasseh, and I am the least in my father's house* (Judges 6:15).

Gideon claimed to come from a poor family. Plus, he thought of himself as the ''least'' in that family. In verse 27 of chapter 6 we read that Gideon took ten of his personal servants and demolished an altar built to the false god Baal. *Ten* of his personal servants? You and I should be so poor! Despair had definitely gone to Gideon's head. But even if he *was* from a poor family, that was certainly no obstacle for God to overcome in working through Gideon to deliver the Israelites from their enemies.

Did the angel give up at this point? No! God's angel was determined to get his message through to Gideon:

> *And the LORD said unto him, Surely I will be*

> *with thee, and thou shalt smite the Midianites as one man* (Judges 6:16).

Notice that this angel was *the* "angel of the LORD" (verse 12) which was probably a pre-incarnate manifestation of the Lord Jesus Himself! Gideon was actually talking to the Lord. Gideon seemed to be getting the picture here that *God* was going to use him to defeat the Midianites. However *weak* Gideon was in his opinion of himself, he was *strong* when it came to speaking with the angel:

> *And he* [Gideon] *said unto him, If now I have found grace in thy sight, then shew me a sign that thou talkest with me* (Judges 6:17).

Gideon asked for a miracle—and got it! He prepared a sacrifice, and the angel of the Lord touched it with his staff. Fire came out of the rock upon which the "flesh and unleavened cakes" laid and devoured them. Finally Gideon " . . . *perceived that he was an angel of the LORD* . . . " (Judges 6:22). Instead of rejoicing, however, Gideon retreated into fear:

> *And when Gideon perceived that he was an angel of the LORD, Gideon said, Alas, O Lord GOD! for because I have seen an angel of the LORD face to face. And the LORD said unto him, Peace be unto thee; fear not: thou shalt not die* (Judges 6:22,23).

Isn't Gideon a lot like you and me? We have to be told over and over again, "Peace; fear not," before the message finally sinks in! That's why it's so important to be *constantly* renewing our minds *with the Word of God*—not the newspaper, not the TV news, not what so-and-so says, but with the Word of God. The more you and I saturate our minds with the truth of God's Word, the more we'll walk *out* of depression and walk into the revelation knowledge of God's love and power working on our behalf. And that's exactly what happened to Gideon—he had a revelation of Jehovah which would cause depression to flee from any man:

> *Then Gideon built an altar there unto the* LORD, *and called it Jehovah-shalom: unto this day it is yet in Ophrah of the Abi-ezrites* (Judges 6:24.)

Shalom has beautiful meanings that imply not only peace but also has the idea of living life at its best. Gideon realized God's presence so strongly that he had peace amidst the storm. Despite the circumstances all around him, despite the hopelessness of the situation, Gideon's depression lifted as he experienced the peace of God.

The revelation of Jehovah as the God of peace wasn't given to Gideon so that he would have some warm, fuzzy feeling. No, God always gives us revelation to *activate* us. The peace in Gideon's heart displaced his depression and enabled him to perform a mighty act of faith:

> *And it came to pass the same night, that the* LORD *said unto him, Take thy father's young bullock, even the second bullock of seven years old, and throw down the altar of Baal that thy father hath, and cut down the grove that is by it: And build an altar unto the LORD thy God upon the top of this rock, in the ordered place, and take the second bullock, and offer a burnt sacrifice with the wood of the grove which thou shalt cut down* (Judges 6:25,26).

Gideon, with his new-found revelation of God, obeyed the Lord. Shortly thereafter word came that the Midianites and the Amalekites were gathered against the Israelites once again—probably because they knew it was harvesttime and the best time to ransack the countryside. But this time things would be different. Gideon became one of the *charismatics* of the book of Judges:

> *But the Spirit of the LORD came upon Gideon, and he blew a trumpet; and Abi-ezer was gathered after him* (Judges 6:34).

In the Hebrew wording Gideon was "clothed in the Spirit." That was a far cry from the unbelief that he had been clothed with earlier! Messengers ran to gather recruits from the tribes of Asher, Zebulun, and Naphtali. A national fervor seemed to sweep the land. Unfortunately, Gideon felt the old fears welling up in his heart. Rather than trust the Lord's speaking in his spirit, Gideon asked for another sign of assurance from God: he put out a fleece overnight and asked that the fleece be wet with dew while the ground around it be dry. When God answered that request, Gideon asked for still another sign: this time the ground would be wet and the fleece would be dry. How patient and merciful the Lord was to answer both requests. Gideon could have been *fleeced by his fleeces*!

God showed Gideon that he wasn't the only one in Israel who was depressed and full of fear. Gideon was told to send home everyone who was fearful—and 22,000 men headed for home! This turn of events could have wiped Gideon out; but his visible miracle, his revelation of Jehovah-shalom, his charismatic experience, and his fleece all undergirded his faith in God's Word. Gideon had finally learned to look at the promises of God instead of the circumstances around him.

Eventually Gideon's band of men was whittled down to 300. After Gideon evaesdropped on his enemy and learned that even *they* knew that Gideon was a winner, God gave him a tremendous victory over the Midianites. The Midianites fled in great haste. The Israelites who had been sent home must have been waiting in the wings; as the Midianites fled, the Israelites came out in great force and strength. Gideon had gone from depressed to undefeatable!

Remember the keys that turned Gideon's depression into victory: (1) He listened to the voice of the Lord through an angel. Are *you* attuned to God's voice, or are you only hearing and seeing the negative circumstances around you? (2) Gideon received a revelation of Jehovah-shalom. Do *you* know the peace of God that comes from renewing your mind to His Word? (3) The Spirit of the Lord came upon Gideon. Are *you* walking in the Spirit daily? Remember too that God is no respecter of persons; He will turn your fear into faith and your depression into a spiritual high!

ANGELS, DEPRESSION, AND ELIJAH

Have you ever thought, "I wish I could just die. God, I don't want to go on another minute; just take my life"? Many of us may have had thoughts like that at one time or another. Depression is one of Satan's tools to take our eyes off the promises of God and put them onto the circumstances around us.

Sometimes we may try to justify our feelings by saying, "But you don't know what I've been through!" You're right. Maybe *I* haven't been through what you've been through. But that doesn't matter. What matters is that *Jesus* has been through worse things than you, and He knows the way out of the worst situation. Jesus has a provision for you in His Word that will overcome depression, grief, and fear.

Elijah was one of Israel's greatest prophets—his character was as strong as iron! But even *he* experienced depression. I want to look with you at how God brought Elijah out of depression and into victory.

Do you remember the story of how Elijah called down fire on his sacrifice to prove that Jehovah was the true God? You'll find the story in I Kings 18. It's an exciting story that you don't want to miss. Elijah stood up to 450 false prophets of Baal and 400 prophets of the groves and experienced the miracle-working power of God in a mighty way. The Bible says that the "hand of the Lord" was upon Elijah. Well, I should say so!

I want you to notice, however, that right after these events Elijah was overcome with depression—to the point of wanting to end his life! Queen Jezebel heard of all that had happened to Elijah, his sacrifice, and the prophets of Baal (Elijah had them all killed!), yet still she refused to repent or change her wicked ways:

> *Then Jezebel sent a messenger unto Elijah, saying, So let the gods do to me, and more also, if I make not thy life as the life of one of them by tomorrow about this time* (I Kings 19:2).

Elijah had just experienced the power of God on his behalf in such an unusual way. It is difficult to understand how he could be afraid of Jezebel's threats knowing that God was on his side. Nevertheless, something snapped in Elijah; and he became fearful and depressed:

> *And when he* [Elijah] *saw that, he arose, and went for his life, and came to Beer-sheba, which belongeth to Judah, and left his servant there. But he himself went a day's journey into the wilderness, and came and sat down under a juniper tree: and he requested for himself that he might die; and said, It is enough; now, O LORD, take away my life; for I am not better than my fathers* (I Kings 19:3,4).

I believe that it is important to notice how fear and depression crept into Elijah's life. He was physically tired at this time. Sometimes the most spiritual thing you can do is to get a good night's sleep! If your body is tired and your brain is tired, that will definitely affect your soul and spirit.

Elijah was tired and hungry. He was downright "out of it." But God didn't chastise him; He didn't say, "Elijah, you've seen so much of the supernatural; and here you are having a pity party and wanting to die. *I'm* the One Who is *tired* of you!" No, no, no. God isn't like that. Instead of being disgusted with Elijah, the Lord sent an angel to minister to him:

> *And as he* [Elijah] *lay and slept under a juniper tree, behold, then an angel touched him, and said unto him, Arise and eat* (I Kings 19:5).

The angel told Elijah to *rise and eat.* If you are depressed today, I believe that the Lord is saying the same thing to you: Arise and eat. He's not telling you to eat ice cream or cookies; He is telling you to eat God's Word. Can I be honest with you? You haven't been eating enough of the Word or you wouldn't be in unbelief and depression in the first place! If you will rise out of your feelings of depression long enough to eat God's Word, the Lord will give you some revelation knowledge and some supernatural things will begin to happen in your life. God has some supernatural things *already* prepared for you just as the angel had something already prepared for Elijah:

> *And he looked, and, behold, there was a cake baken on the coals, and a cruse of water at his head. And he did eat and drink, and laid him down again* (I Kings 19:6).

God is the God Who has seen ahead and made a provision for *you*. He has the Bread of life and the water of life to meet your every need. Don't look at what you've been through; look at what God can take you through. No matter how depressed you've been or how long it's been, it's not too late to start eating and drinking spiritual food that will give you the strength to carry on.

"But Marilyn," you say, "I just can't do it." You're right! You're right! And that's just what the angel said to Elijah:

> *And the angel of the LORD came again the second time, and touched him, and said, Arise and eat: because the journey is too great for thee* (I Kings 19:7).

All your problems are too great for you! You were never meant to overcome them alone. That's why God has ministering angels! If you will follow their advice, you will have renewed strength. Elijah did, and two meals kept him going for 40 days and nights:

> *And he arose, and did eat and drink, and went in the strength of that meat forty days and forty nights unto Horeb the mount of God* (I Kings 19:8).

If you will eat and drink God's Word, the Lord will take

you to places of fresh inspiration that you have never even imagined! God gave Elijah fresh inspiration; only this time it wasn't in the way of something spectacular or outwardly supernatural. This time the Lord brought inspiration to Elijah through a still small voice:

> *And he* [God] *said, Go forth, and stand upon the mount before the LORD. And, behold, the LORD passed by, and a great and strong wind rent the mountains, and brake in pieces the rocks before the LORD; but the LORD was not in the wind: and after the wind an earthquake; but the LORD was not in the earthquake: And after the earthquake a fire; but the LORD was not in the fire: and after the fire a still small voice. And it was so, when Elijah heard it, that he wrapped his face in his mantel, and went out, . . .* (I Kings 19:11-13).

Elijah was still having a pity party when he arrived at Horeb; he was whining about being the only one who loved God. He should have known better; he had seen the Israelites slay the 450 prophets of Baal. It's easy to be deceived when you're depressed. But the Lord had a wonderful way of encouraging Elijah; God said, "I'm not through with you yet!"

Doesn't it feel good to be wanted, to be needed? You're right! And the Lord wanted Elijah to anoint Hazael to be king over Syria, to anoint Jehu to be the new king over Israel, and to anoint Elisha as Elijah's replacement (see I Kings 19:15,16). In addition to those assignments, the Lord let Elijah know that there were 7,000 others in Israel who had not worshiped the false god Baal. Elijah never whined again!

Have *you* been whining? Have you thrown a pity party where you were the only one who came? God has some wonderful news to encourage you and pull you out of your depression: the Lord isn't finished with you yet! If you still have breath, God wants to use you. His anointing can still flow through you.

It's time for *your* depression to come to an end in the name of Jesus! God can use you, whether you are the "least" of your family (as Gideon thought of himself) or whether you have become burned out (like Elijah). The Lord has seen ahead and made a provision for you; the next step is yours. It's time for you to *rise and eat* and receive fresh inspiration.

Chapter Seven

ANGELS AND YOUR PROTECTION

"My heart began to pound uncontrollably as I realized that I was being followed by two men. A stopover on a bus trip from Los Angeles to Chicago had left me with extra time on my hands, so I had decided to take a little walk outside the bus terminal just before dawn. I panicked when I became lost and heard footsteps behind me. 'Why do they always have to put bus terminals in the worst part of every town?' I thought to myself.

"Our pastor had preached a sermon about *guardian angels* not too long before this trip. It meant little to me at the time, but now his words came back to remind me of the protection that God had made available to His children.

"'Dear God,' I prayed, 'if there *are* such things as guardian angels, I really need one now.' My faith felt terribly small! As I turned a corner, my heart sank as I saw *another* man walking down the street toward me. 'God help me,' I sighed. And then I noticed that *this* man looked as if he was dressed for work in a suit and tie.

"'Sir, I'm lost and two men are following me. Please, I'm trying to find the bus terminal.'

"'Follow me,' he said as he led me the few blocks to the station where my bus awaited me. I never saw the other two men again.

"I thanked him, and I thanked the Lord for sending me someone at just the right time. I was too embarrassed to ask him if he was an angel—but as far as I'm concerned, God had sent a guardian 'angel' in answer to my prayer!"

This woman's encounter was not an isolated experience. The Bible informs us that God has appointed angels to minister to the heirs of salvation:

> *But to which of the angels said he at any time, Sit on my right hand, until I make thine enemies thy footstool? Are they not all ministering spirits, sent forth to minister for them who shall be heirs of salvation?* (Hebrews 1:13,14).

Angels have been "sent forth to minister." Isn't that good news? They are not just standing around watching what's going on in your life; they are here *to minister* to your needs. King David knew about the activity of angels; he even knew that angels go "camping" with you:

> *The angel of the LORD encampeth round about them that fear him, and delivereth them* (Psalms 34:7).

Angels are sent to deliver you and me. We can count on their help when needed. Angels have specific duties:

> *For he shall give his angels charge over thee, to keep thee in all thy ways. They shall bear thee up in their hands, lest thou dash thy foot against a stone* (Psalms 91:11,12).

Angels are your attendants. They have been assigned to take care of you, to keep you safe in all your ways. Anyone who comes against you must give account to your guardian angel:

> *Take heed that ye despise not one of these little ones; for I say unto you, That in heaven their angels do always behold the face of my Father which is in heaven* (Matthew 18:10).

Angels give a report to God the Father concerning each

and every Christian. But they are not just *reporters.* No, they receive assignments from God based upon their reports. Sometimes their assignments may include rescuing a woman who is lost in a strange city; or, as in the case of Daniel in the Old Testament, their assignment may include an overnight stay in the lion's den!

DANIEL AND HIS GUARDIAN ANGEL

Angels are sent to believers to take care of the *lions* in their lives. Peter tells us who the BIGGEST lion is:

> *Be sober, be vigilant; because your adversary the devil, as a roaring lion, walketh about, seeking whom he may devour* (I Peter 5:8).

Daniel was a man who *literally* looked a lion in the mouth—and lived to tell about it. The name *Daniel* means "God is my judge," and Daniel lived up to his name by trusting a righteous God Who judged Daniel innocent and sent His angel to shut the mouths of several hungry lions.

Daniel was not a young man when he encountered his lions. He probably was in his nineties. He had been taken captive into Babylon when he was just a teenager. Daniel purposed in his heart to stand uncompromisingly on God's Word. He had learned, long beforehand, to pray God's promises rather than his own problems. The time to prepare for lions is *before* you meet one!

There are some "lions" in your future. Count on them! And take the time to prepare for them NOW. Follow Daniel's example, and you'll be fully prepared for any emergency.

Second only to the king, Daniel was a *big wheel* in the Persian empire. He was the first of three presidents who ruled over the 120 ruling princes of Persia. Notice why Daniel was preferred over all the others:

> *Then this Daniel was preferred above the presidents and princes, because an excellent spirit was in him; and the king thought to set him over the whole realm* (Daniel 6:3).

Men looking on would have said that Daniel was a Jewish boy who made it big because he had power, wealth, and favor. However, the Bible tells us the real reason for Daniel's high position was his "excellent spirit." This caused the 120 princes to be envious, and they sought to find cause to accuse Daniel of wrongdoing against the king.

The accusers found Daniel to be faithful to the king. But they also knew that Daniel was faithful to his God, and so they looked for something in Daniel's spiritual life that they could use to trap him. Daniel's prayer life became the object of their scheme. It was well known that Daniel prayed three times each day:

> *Now when Daniel knew that the writing was signed, he went into his house; and his windows being open in his chamber toward Jerusalem, he kneeled upon his knees three times a day, and prayed, and gave thanks before his God, as he did aforetime* (Daniel 6:10).

The presidents and the princes devised a plan which they felt would please the king and, ultimately, would remove Daniel from the scene. They persuaded King Darius to pass a decree that no prayer should be prayed to anyone but the king for a period of 30 days. The penalty for breaking the decree was to be thrown into a den of lions. Once the decree was signed, according to Persian law, it could never be revoked.

The decree didn't stop Daniel from following his daily practice of prayer. However, the prayer that resulted in Daniel being thrown into the lions' den was the same prayer that saved his life! It wasn't necessary for Daniel to *prepare* to meet the lions; he lived a life of prayer that prepared him for anything and everything that came his way. The book of Daniel gives us a glimpse of his prayer life. Daniel prayed earnestly:

> *And I set my face unto the Lord God, to seek by prayer and supplications, with fasting, and sackcloth, and ashes* (Daniel 9:3).

Daniel prayed desperately:

> *In those days I Daniel was mourning three full weeks. I ate no pleasant bread, neither came flesh nor wine in my mouth, neither did I anoint myself at all, till three whole weeks were fulfilled* (Daniel 10:2,3).

Daniel prayed powerfully:

> *Then said he unto me, Fear not, Daniel: for from the first day that thou didst set thine heart to understand, and to chasten thyself before thy God, thy words were heard, and I am come for thy words* (Daniel 10:12).

Once it was known that Daniel had broken the king's decree, no one could deliver Daniel from the den of lions, not even the king who passed the decree. The king saw through the trap that had been laid for Daniel, but he was powerless to change his own law. However, the king knew of Daniel's life of prayer and commitment to the true God. He expressed confidence that Daniel's God would deliver him:

> *Then the king commanded, and they brought Daniel, and cast him into the den of lions. Now the king spake and said unto Daniel, Thy God whom thou servest continually, he will deliver thee* (Daniel 6:16).

And deliver He did! Early the next morning, the king called to Daniel in the darkness of that den; and to his joy and surprise the strong voice of Daniel answered:

> *Then said Daniel unto the king, O king, live for ever. My God hath sent his angel, and hath shut the lions' mouths, that they have not hurt me: forasmuch as before him innocency was found in me; and also before thee, O king, have I done no hurt* (Daniel 6:21,22).

Sometimes we want God to protect us in a time of crisis; but until we repent of sin, we shouldn't *expect* supernatural protection. We can't live a life of sin and lukewarmness and then complain about the lack of supernatural deliverance in our lives. Daniel was confident of God's protection because Daniel was in a right relationship with his heavenly Father.

It was an amazing feat the angel performed for Daniel. But there is no indication that Daniel was amazed at all; he was fully prepared for the "lions" that would come into his life. Angels will act as guardians in *your* life also, if you have prepared yourself. Let me give you a list of things to do NOW to prepare for any future overnight stay in the lion's den:

1. Read your Bible *before* you arrive in the lions' den.
2. Have a disciplined prayer time *before* the lions line up at your door.
3. Keep your focus on the Word of God during a crisis.

4. Keep an excellent spirit at all times.
5. Have faith that the Word will work for you.
6. Look to God for your deliverance.
7. Give God the glory for your deliverance.

MY GUARDIAN ANGEL AT WORK

One cold, snowy night many years back I had an experience with that old lion, the devil; and the Lord sent my guardian angel just in the nick of time! I had finished dinner for my family and was looking forward to a relaxing evening at home alone with our family pet poodle, Beethoven.

My husband and son had gone to an oil-painting lesson, and my daughter had gone to her piano lesson. It was so rare for me to have such a private evening, and I would savor every moment of it. There was that new cake recipe I had been wanting to try, and what better time than now! I began to gather all the ingredients together; and while running up the stairs to find an apron, I heard the bedroom phone ringing, interrupting the peaceful silence I had been enjoying. Hastily, I picked up the phone, answering questions in rapid-fire yeses and nos, waiting for the conversation to end so that I could get back to my evening alone.

Beethoven stretched out at my feet in a leisurely fashion while I talked. He was in no hurry, just wanting to be where I was. After about ten minutes, I said goodbye to the caller and hurriedly walked down the stairs to get on with my cake baking. I had kicked off my shoes while talking on the phone, so I hastened down the stairs in my stocking feet. As I sauntered into the kitchen, a cold draft swept over my feet and I noticed the back door was wide open. My first thought was, ''Which of my children forgot to shut the door?'' And yet I knew in my heart that no one in the family would leave the door open on such a cold, wintry night.

While I was pondering, my little poodle, Beethoven, rushed over to the wrought iron fence separating our family room from our kitchen. (The family room is a level lower than the kitchen, with the wrought iron rail used as a divider between the two rooms.) The family room was dark, but Beethoven was aware of more than just the darkness; he let out a low, throaty growl. Every little black curly hair on his body seemed to be electrified. He was poised, ready to jump right through the iron railing.

By now, he and I both felt a strange ''presence'' in the darkness of that room. Who could this uninvited guest possibly be, and was he or she dangerous? I always wondered about my reactions in the time of emergency. Should I scream? Run out the back door? Go into the dark family room and chase out the intruder? As these thoughts raced through my mind, it was as though someone took my arm and guided me to close the back door and lock it.

A calmness, quite beyond description, filled my spirit, my mind, and even my body. Every movement I made seemed effortless, as though each motion had already been planned and I was simply walking in steps placed before me. I picked up our tiny poodle and walked out the front door. When my stocking feet touched the cold concrete, I suddenly wished I had gone back up those stairs and put on my shoes. I walked rapidly, then began to run across the lawn to our neighbors' house. I felt no embarrassment about taking my problem to them, since my husband had come to their daughter's rescue in a similar circumstance.

As I stood shivering on their front porch waiting for them to answer the door, I probed my mind, trying to imagine who could be this frightening, mysterious intruder? I felt the warmth of Beethoven's furry body in my arms, the only spot of warmth on my whole body. Even my mind seemed to be numb with cold. At last my neighbor came to the door. He looked at me as though I had lost my mind—no shoes, no coat, and holding a dog! Before he could open his mouth, I opened mine. The words flew out, "There's someone in my house, hiding! They came in the back door. Would you please come over to my house with me?"

I waited with my feet almost numb with cold as he grabbed a jacket and flashlight. The two of us cut across the lawn. I noticed the moon, and for a second it seemed like a normal, cold, Colorado night. Suddenly, because of the brightness of the moon, we could easily see a figure bursting through my front door, running in long strides and jumping into a car parked not too far from the front of my house.

Though I could tell that the figure was tall, maybe five feet ten or eleven inches, I was not certain it was a male. Much of the movement was like a woman. I felt a sickening feeling in my stomach as I realized I could easily identify my unwelcomed intruder; she was a large woman who had many mental problems and extremely hostile reactions. The pastors of our church had spent many hours counseling with her and had encouraged her to seek a special Christian counseling service. She had refused that and psychiatric help as well.

Why had she waited until my family was gone? Why had she hidden in some dark corner of our family room? What did she want? What were her intentions? I cannot give you positive answers to these questions, but I do know this: my guardian angel was very busy that night. I believe that he personally took my arm and guided me and calmed me in those first moments of panic.

When my husband came home with our daughter and son, they walked in the front door to the delicious aroma of a freshly baked pound cake. My husband asked, "Why is every light on in this house?" My neighbor had insisted upon going through every room and closet in the house, turning on all the lights! He had also called the police, but I didn't tell my husband about the intruder and my guardian angel until *after* cake and coffee!

To this day, I can honestly attest to the fact that the rescue squad of heaven—God's angels—had come to my aid, turning what might have been a tragedy into a beautiful testimony of angelic visitation. I am so glad that the Lord's angels "camped" around my house that evening.

GUARDIANS OF THE ISRAELITES

I doubt that Israel had any idea just how much God was protecting them as they traveled through the wilderness. The Egyptian Pharaoh was after them. He had come with his chariots, and the whole nation of Israel was backed up against the Red Sea. They had nowhere to go but into the water! But God was protecting them, and He used an angel to do it:

> *And the angel of God, which went before the camp of Israel, removed and went behind them; and the pillar of the cloud went from before their*

face, and stood behind them: And it came between the camp of the Egyptians and the camp of Israel; and it was a cloud and darkness to them, but it gave light by night to these: so that the one came not near the other all the night (Exodus 14:19,20).

What did this angel do? He came up behind the Israelites and protected them from the Egyptian army. The cloud that the angel controlled was dark on the Egyptian side and bright, like the glory of God, toward the Israelites.

The angel was sent to protect God's people, perhaps as many as seven million men, women, boys, and girls. Does God have enough angels for that many people? I don't think it's a problem at all. Remember, only one-third of the angels fell with Satan; that leaves two-thirds left who are appointed to the household of faith.

We read about the same angel again when God delivered the Ten Commandments and the ceremonial laws and ordinances to the Israelites:

Behold, I send an Angel before thee, to keep thee in the way, and to bring thee into the place which I have prepared (Exodus 23:20).

The angel who protected them from Pharaoh's army would be the same one who would take them safely through the wilderness—if they obeyed the angel:

But if thou shalt indeed obey his [the angel's] *voice, and do all that I speak; then I will be an enemy unto thine enemies, and an adversary unto thine adversaries* (Exodus 23:22).

The Lord spoke of the angel again when He urged Moses to take the Israelites into the Promised Land:

Therefore now go, lead the people unto the

> *place of which I have spoken unto thee: . . .* (Exodus 32:34).

A guardian angel was with the Israelites when they left Egypt, when they were in the wilderness, and when they went into the Promised Land. This angel was anything but a "fair-weather friend." He was with the Israelites during their most difficult times. Angels *work* for the household of faith; they don't just sit around as spectators.

God renewed His promise to the nation of Israel one more time. Do you think that something is important if God mentions it *four* times? You're right! The fourth time God mentioned the angel, we see just how *active* the angel was going to be:

> *And I will send an angel before thee; and I will drive out the Canaanite, the Amorite, and the Hittite, and the Perizzite, the Hivite, and the Jebusite* (Exodus 33:2).

When we obey God's Word, angels will fight for us! Not all angels have harps; some have heavenly *boxing gloves.* Your guardian angels are fighting for you, protecting you in ways you may never be aware of. The Israelites had all those other "ites" to drive out of the Promised Land before they could settle down in peace. You and I also have our "ites" to conquer before we can find peace.

There is no peace when you are barely making it from paycheck to paycheck each week or each month; but angels can bring you money from unexpected sources or even give you creative ideas for making your money stretch further or for earning more money in less time.

There is no peace when you are struggling with a health problem that refuses to go away. But angels can nourish your physical body and strengthen your spirit man. God's angels are assigned to watch over you and take care of you in every way; they are before you and behind you to guard you from your enemies.

GUARDIAN ANGELS AND JACOB

It's one thing for God to assign an angel to watch over a whole nation like Israel, but do you know that God also is interested in individuals? Jacob is a good case in point. When he left his father and his mother to flee his brother Esau, God gave him a vision filled with angels:

> *And he dreamed, and behold a ladder set up on the earth, and the top of it reached to heaven: and behold the angels of God ascending and descending on it* (Genesis 28:12).

Jacob was encouraged by the dream to know that God's presence was with him as he journeyed. The Lord spoke to Jacob and promised to keep him safe wherever he traveled. Jacob called the place where he had the vision of the angels the "house of God." God's house today is composed of born-again Christians. Are *you* born again? Then you are a part of God's house, and there are angels in that house to guard and protect you as you travel!

When Jacob returned to the Promised Land, the Lord sent angels to go before him:

> *And Jacob went on his way, and the angels of God met him. And when Jacob saw them, he said, This is God's host: and he called the name of that place Mahanaim* (Genesis 32:1,2).

Mahanaim means "two bands." God had sent two whole bands of angels to accompany Jacob. Do you think that you would feel safe knowing that there were two companies of angels traveling with you? Jacob probably thought, "Thank You, Lord; this is just what I need in case my brother Esau still wants to kill me for stealing his blessing!" Jacob had angels before him and angels behind him to protect, guard, and prepare his way.

One of the most difficult things for anyone who works is to go into the boss' office and ask for a raise. Is there any way to make it easier? Yes! Pray and ask the Lord to send His angels before you to prepare the way. If you've been diligent in your work and faithful to your company, you have every right to expect your angel to go before you and work on your behalf.

A man I'll call Edward had worked for a company for some time without a raise. He and his wife prayed about what he could do. His boss was not a Christian and, in fact, was antagonistic about Edward's stand for Christ in the office. Edward's wife said, "Let's pray that when you go into your boss' office, God will have prepared his heart to hear what you have to say and to consider your raise based only upon your abilities."

They prayed, and the Lord impressed Edward to make his appeal early during a Monday morning. Monday morning came, and Edward asked for angels to go before him to remove any antagonism that would prevent his boss from giving him a fair hearing.

"It was amazing," Edward reported to his wife. "He was *very* friendly, and we had a wonderful time talking about the company's future plans and where I would fit into those plans."

Did he get the raise? "I didn't get *exactly* what I had hoped and prayed for, but I did get a raise. More importantly, I think my boss and I have more respect for each other. I really believe that God sent His angel before me to smooth the way.''

GUARDIAN ANGELS AND ELISHA

One of the most unique accounts of guardian angels in the Old Testament is found in II Kings. Syria was at war with Israel, but the Israelites knew their every move. The king of Syria was frustrated, thinking that surely there must be a spy in his court:

> *Therefore the heart of the king of Syria was sore troubled for this thing; and he called his servants, and said unto them, Will ye not shew me which of us is for the king of Israel?* (II Kings 6:11).

His servants assured him that there were no spies in his court. ''King, Israel has a prophet named Elisha; and he hears from God. Elisha somehow hears even the words that you speak in your bedchamber! Elisha is the problem, Sir.''

At the time, Elisha was living in a little town called Dothan. The king of Syria sent a large part of his army down to Dothan and surrounded the entire city at night. Imagine what the inhabitants of that city thought when they awakened to find the Syrian army surrounding their puny city! Elisha's servant must have been one of the first to get up that morning:

> *And when the servant of the man of God was risen early, and gone forth, behold, an host compassed the city both with horses and chariots. And his servant said unto him, Alas, my master! how shall we do?* (II Kings 6:15).

Elisha's servant probably got up early to have his *morning devotions.* He may even have prayed and thanked the Lord for his daily bread and for his safety! But when the light of dawn revealed the Syrian army, the servant's faith went out the window.

Has that ever happened to you? It seems that the times when our faith is tested the most is right after we've experienced the sweet presence of the Lord. When my children were very young, it seemed like Sunday mornings were the devil's biggest time to cause us to "lose our faith." My husband and I would get up early to spend time with the Lord. The house was quiet, and it felt like heaven as I spent time meditating in the Word and praying.

But when the sun came up, and it was time for getting the kids dressed, sitting down to breakfast, and getting to church on time, I'd want to pull my hair out. Everything went wrong! I couldn't find the right socks to match a pair of trousers for my son, or I couldn't find my daughter's hairbrush. Just before we were ready to leave, someone would remember that we hadn't put the dog outside all morning. By the time we were rushing down the freeway to church, I'd think to myself, "Lord, where are You?"

That might be what happened to Elisha's servant. He was up early to pray and build up his faith; but when he saw the army of Syria on every side, he said, "Lord, where are You?" The servant ran to Elisha and said, "Master, what are we going to do?"

Now, it's obvious that Elisha didn't need to get "prayed up" for a time of crisis. He *stayed* prayed up; he stayed in the presence of the Lord at all times. That's what you and I need to do—stay prayed up at all times so that the devil doesn't have a chance to roll over us.

Elisha knew that God's army of guardian angels was constantly on duty around him. Elisha didn't physically need to see the angels who were sent to guard him; but for his servant's sake, Elisha prayed for the Lord to open his servant's eyes to see God's guardian angels:

> *And Elisha prayed, and said,* LORD, *I pray thee, open his eyes, that he may see. And the* LORD *opened the eyes of the young man; and he saw: and, behold, the mountain was full of horses and chariots of fire round about Elisha* (II Kings 6:17).

Elisha knew an important truth that you and I need always to remember:

> . . . *Fear not: for they that be with us are more than they that be with them* (II Kings 6:16).

Whatever your situation, whatever your crisis, whatever your "impossible" circumstances might *appear* to be, there are more angels working for you than there are demon spirits working against you. And that goes for your spouse and your children too. Pray that God will open *your* eyes to see the angelic forces that are arrayed in your behalf. They are sent to fight for you and for your family.

Elisha prayed and asked God for another miracle. This time Elisha asked God to blind the Syrian troops. God answered that prayer too, and Elisha led the whole army away from the city of Dothan to the city of Samaria where they were fed and eventually sent back unharmed to Syria! Was Elisha nuts? No, God had given him wisdom in handling the Syrian army. Now that the Syrians knew how *nice* the Israelites were, the Bible says " . . . *the bands of Syria came no more into the land of Israel*" (II Kings 6:23).

Both of these miracles occurred at *Dothan,* which means ''double feast.'' God's angels will prepare a *double feast* for you and your loved ones when the occasion is needed. *Your* part is to stay prayed up and to continue living in the Lord's presence.

God is not always so *gracious* to those, like the Syrians, who oppose Him. Angels are sometimes the agents of God's justice upon unbelievers *and* believers. In the next chapter we'll see how angels are used as instruments of judgment!

Chapter Eight

ANGELS AND JUDGMENT

It is popular to picture angels as cute little babies with chubby legs and arms, flying about with arrows that infect their recipients with a dose of "love" that knocks them off their feet! As we have seen, nothing could be further from the truth. Angels are mighty beings who respond to God's commands; they rescue God's people from hopeless situations, they give direction and guidance to those who are lost, and they protect the faithful from certain danger.

There is another side to angelic activity that seldom gets attention: angels are instruments of God's judgment. An African folk tale illustrates this point well:

> In a tribal village there once lived four men, each with a particular limitation. The first was blind, the second couldn't hear, the third was lame, and the fourth man was a beggar. To this village came an angel in disguise. The angel asked each man what he wanted most.
>
> Naturally the blind man replied, "My sight!" The deaf man wanted his hearing, while the lame man wanted the use of his legs. The beggar asked for money to feed and clothe his family.
>
> To their surprise, the stranger granted each of their wishes. The men, in return, thanked the stranger and vowed never to forget his kindness.
>
> Years later the angel returned. When the man who had been blind saw him, he thought, "He's probably come back to ask for money just because he did me a little favor." When the angel

asked him how he was doing, the man who had received his sight answered, ''Not well; I have to do everything for myself now. Nobody will help me anymore.''

''Very well,'' replied the angel, ''then you shall have your blindness back.'' And with that the man became blind again.

The man who had been deaf had a similar attitude when he saw the angel. ''How is it to be able to hear?'' asked the angel. ''Oh, it has its disadvantages,'' complained the man. ''So many sounds get on my nerves and keep me awake at night.''

''Very well,'' replied the angel, ''then you shall have your hearing taken away from you.'' And the man was deaf once again!

The lame man, too, was suspicious of the angel. ''He probably wants *me* to do something for him just because he helped me a long time ago. Well, I'm too busy so I won't!''

When the angel asked him how he liked using his legs, the man replied, ''I can't run very fast, and at night they sometimes ache.'' And he suddenly found himself lame once again.

The angel finally visited the man who had been a beggar. He now lived in a beautiful house and dressed in fine clothes. The angel knocked on the door and asked for a drink of water. Although the man didn't recognize the angel, he invited him in and asked him to stay for dinner.

''Why are you so kind?'' asked the angel. ''Because years ago someone helped me when

> I was poor, and now I show my gratitude by helping others,'' the man answered.
>
> ''Very well,'' the angel replied. ''You shall keep your wealth!''

This same angel brought blessing and calamity—a principle that is abundantly supported by the Bible. God's mercy and love are extended to those who seek Him with all their hearts; but for those who turn their backs on Him, God's wrath can have devastating results! And angels are God's agents in *both* instances.

ANGELS WHO BLESS AND CURSE

Early in the Bible, in the nineteenth chapter of Genesis, we read about two angels who were sent by God to bring blessing and cursing. The story involves Abraham and his nephew Lot. The Lord appeared to Abraham and let him in on a secret—He was going to destroy the cities of Sodom and Gomorrah:

> *And the LORD said, Because the cry of Sodom and Gomorrah is great, and because their sin is very grievous; And Abraham drew near, and said, Wilt thou also destroy the righteous with the wicked?* (Genesis 18:20,23).

Abraham was concerned for his nephew Lot. Lot had chosen to live in a horrible place. Sodom and Gomorrah were known for the immorality practiced by their inhabitants. Homosexuality was rampant and openly practiced by the men of those cities. Abraham pleaded with the Lord to spare Lot and his family, and the Lord agreed. Two angels were sent to bless Lot and his family. For Lot, the angels were *guardian angels* sent to protect him. For the ungodly citizens of Sodom and Gomorrah, the angels were *destroying angels* sent to curse the cities:

> *. . . we will destroy this place, because the cry of them is waxen great before the face of the LORD; and the LORD hath sent us to destroy it* (Genesis 19:13).

The angels, however, could not destroy the cities until they had rescued Lot and those with him:

> *Haste thee, escape thither; for I cannot do any thing till thou be come thither . . .* (Genesis 19:22).

Once the guardian angels had warned and practically *pushed* Lot, his wife, and their two daughters out of town, God's judgment fell from the skies:

> *Then the LORD rained upon Sodom and upon Gomorrah brimstone and fire from the LORD out of heaven* (Genesis 19:24).

Angels can bring deliverance and they can help bring about God's judgment. Lot was blessed to have someone who prayed for him. The prayer of intercession saved Lot's life. Is there an individual at your church who is praying constantly for your family? Are *you* praying for the other families in your church? We need to have godly men and women praying for us and our children, and we need to lift up our friends and relatives to the LORD. It's a two-way street!

ANGELS AND PHARAOH'S CHARIOTS

There's an interesting verse in Exodus which seems to indicate that God's angels stripped the wheels off Pharaoh's chariots! The Egyptians pursued the Israelites when Pharaoh had a change of heart about letting all his slave labor go free. The Israelites found themselves trapped between Pharaoh's 600 chariots and the Red Sea.

God's angel took up his position behind the people, and the Lord separated the Israelites from the Egyptians with a cloud:

> *And the angel of God, which went before the camp of Israel, removed and went behind them; and the pillar of the cloud went from before their face, and stood behind them: And it came between the camp of the Egyptians and the camp of Israel; and it was a cloud and darkness to them, but it gave light by night to these: so that the one came not near the other all the night* (Exodus 14:19,20).

The cloud was dark on the side facing the Egyptians and light on the side of the Israelites. That light allowed the entire nation to see the mighty miracles God worked on their behalf: the waters of the Red Sea parted, enabling the Israelites to walk over the dry sea bed to the other shore.

Pharaoh must have thought, "Well, if it works for them, it will work for me." But it didn't:

> *And it came to pass, that in the morning watch the LORD looked unto the host of the Egyptians through the pillar of fire and of the cloud, and troubled the host of the Egyptians, And took off their chariot wheels, that they drave them heavily: so that the Egyptians said, Let us flee from the face of Israel; for the LORD fighteth for them against the Egyptians* (Exodus 14:24,25).

I think the Lord has a good sense of humor, don't you? I think that angels knocked those wheels off. The

Egyptians couldn't drive their chariots because the wheels somehow kept falling off. They hadn't done that before on the long pursuit of the Israelites. God assigned His angels the task of loosening the bolts on those wheels. The angels were used to help bring about God's judgment upon Pharaoh.

THE ANGEL WHO KILLED 185,000 SOLDIERS

Around 725 years before Christ, the northern ten tribes of Israel were taken into captivity by the Assyrians. The northern tribes had turned their backs upon God and were committing terrible sins. The land was left desolate; it was a desperate time. Thousands of men, women, and children were killed by the Assyrians. The time was coming, however, when God would judge the Assyrians. The angel of the Lord would destroy 185,000 of Assyria's finest fighting men.

The king of Assyria had conquered all of the known civilized world at that time—except the two little tribes called Judah to the south. Do you think that if you were living in Judah, you might just be a little scared when you heard that Assyria was on its way to wipe out the final tiny tribes that stood in its way of complete conquest?

Sennacherib, the king of Assyria, sent one of his ministers (Rabshakeh) to Jerusalem to demand Hezekiah's surrender. Rabshakeh tried to scare the people who had gathered along the walls of Jerusalem into surrender:

> *Hearken not to Hezekiah: for thus saith the king of Assyria, Make an agreement with me by a present, and come out to me: and eat ye every*

> *one of his vine, and every one of his fig tree, and drink ye every one the waters of his own cistern; Beware lest Hezekiah persuade you, saying, The* LORD *will deliver us. Hath any of the gods of the nations delivered his land out of the hand of the king of Assyria?* (Isaiah 36:16,18).

Rabshakeh lumped the true God of Israel in with the false gods of other nations. The Lord was slandered and insulted—not a very smart thing to do! But Hezekiah had ordered his people to keep their mouths shut:

> *But they held their peace, and answered him not a word: for the king's commandment was, saying, Answer him not* (Isaiah 36:21).

Have you ever been in a situation like that? Someone has just insulted you or someone you know, and your first response is to verbally slap them right back in the face! The next time that happens, remember Hezekiah's advice and *bite your tongue.* Sometimes silence is the best weapon for staying out of trouble:

> *Be not rash with thy mouth, and let not thine heart be hasty to utter any thing before God: for God is in heaven, and thou upon earth: therefore let thy words be few* (Ecclesiastes 5:2).

In a time of crisis, it is important to restrict what we say. During World War II there was a saying that "Loose lips sink ships." The same is true when we're involved in a war of words. Wait for God's answer to those who insult you or slander you; that's what Hezekiah did:

> *And it came to pass, when king Hezekiah heard it, that he rent his clothes, and covered himself with sackcloth, and went into the house of the* LORD (Isaiah 37:1).

What did Hezekiah do when his crisis hit? Did he say, "Well, I am going to skip church this weekend; and I am going to the mountains to have some fun so that I can get my mind off of my problems"? No, that's not what he did. *He went to church.*

Some people think that they can be Christians two days each year—Easter and Christmas—and still be victorious when a crisis hits their family. But you cannot play loose and free with God and expect to see the miraculous.

Not only did Hezekiah go to church, but he also sent for spiritual help:

> *And he* [Hezekiah] *sent Eliakim, who was over the household, and Shebna the scribe, and the elders of the priests covered with sackcloth, unto Isaiah the prophet the son of Amoz* (Isaiah 37:2).

What do you need when you're in trouble? You don't need ungodly people patting you on the back, telling you that it will be all right. No, they can't help you with anything; they don't know God. When you need the supernatural intervention of God, you won't find it by going to your worldly friends.

Hezekiah knew someone who was spiritual, someone who could be a genuine help in time of need. Do you have such a friend? God has put spiritual people in the church to help the weak when a crisis hits. Take inventory of your friends; is there anyone on the list who is rock solid with God? Is there anyone you can call on in the day of trouble? Hezekiah knew who to call upon, and he knew exactly what needed to be done:

> *And they said unto him* [Isaiah], *Thus saith Hezekiah, This day is a day of trouble, and of rebuke, and of blasphemy: for the children are*

come to the birth, and there is not strength to bring forth. It may be the LORD thy God will hear the words of Rabshakeh, whom the king of Assyria his master hath sent to reproach the living God, and will reprove the words which the LORD thy God hath heard: wherefore lift up thy prayer for the remnant that is left (Isaiah 37:3,4).

In the day of trouble we need spiritual people to pray for us. Isaiah did pray, and God told Hezekiah that Assyria was going to have a "blast"—but it wasn't going to be a party! Rabshakeh heard a rumor of trouble back home, and he was forced to withdraw from the countryside around Jerusalem.

"Don't think you're getting off the hook," Rabshakeh told Hezekiah. "Your God can't help you; I'll be back."

Rabshakeh put his threats into a letter and sent it to Hezekiah. Did Hezekiah wilt at the new threat? No! He took the letter and went again into the Temple, spreading the letter before the Lord. Hezekiah prayed over the letter, and his prayer is a good model for you and me when a crisis hits:

O LORD of hosts, God of Israel, that dwellest between the cherubims, thou art the God, even thou alone, of all the kingdoms of the earth: thou hast made heaven and earth (Isaiah 37:16).

What was the first thing that Hezekiah prayed? Did he pray the problem? No! The first words out of his mouth acknowledged that God was sovereign commander and ruler over all the earth. When a crisis hits, it's important that we have a proper perspective which enables us to *see the bigger picture.* Next, Hezekiah appealed to God's honor:

> *Incline thine ear, O LORD, and hear; open thine eyes, O LORD, and see: and hear all the words of Sennacherib, which hath sent to reproach the living God* (Isaiah 37:17).

Hezekiah knew better than to identify the problem as *his* problem. Sennacherib was defying the "living God," not Hezekiah. When problems come into your life, don't take them personally. If you are a believer in the Lord Jesus Christ, you are not alone! Jesus *in you* will not desert you in a time of crisis. You do not have to face adversity in your own strength. When trouble comes against you, remember that it is also coming against Christ in you; and together you and the Lord are invincible.

Some people think that the Christian's approach to adversity is nothing more than "positive thinking." But notice that Hezekiah wasn't ignoring the facts of his situation:

> *Of a truth, LORD, the kings of Assyria have laid waste all the nations, and their countries, And have cast their gods into the fire: for they were no gods, but the work of men's hands, wood and stone: therefore they have destroyed them* (Isaiah 37:18,19).

Hezekiah knew the hard cold facts of what had happened to the other nations as the cruel Assyrians overran their cities: they were demolished! Sennacherib had tried to convince Judah's king that the same fate awaited him and his people. Hezekiah refused to stick his head in the sand and ignore the Assyrians. He knew the facts, but he also knew something the Assyrians didn't:

> *Now therefore, O LORD our God, save us from his hand, that all the kingdoms of the earth may*

> *know that thou art the* L*ORD*, *even thou only* (Isaiah 37:20).

The other nations had worshiped false gods which could not save them in the time of crisis. Hezekiah knew that this time the Assyrians were up against the true God; and *this time* things would be different!

Can you confidently follow Hezekiah's example in the time of crisis? Are you in the habit of going to the house of the Lord, or do you worship the *god of nature* or the *god of sports* on Sundays? If so, then you will crash in the time of trouble because your ''gods'' won't be able to help you. NOW is the time to be building up your faith in the Almighty God. Now is the time to develop friendships with those who know how to pray, with those who will intercede for you when a crisis hits. Hezekiah went into the Temple, prayed, and called upon Isaiah to pray for God's supernatural intervention.

That night, Hezekiah went to bed with renewed faith in God's Word. God's Word had never failed in his life and would not fail him now.

ONE NIGHT'S WORK

The night was dark with just a sliver of silver light from the moon. There were few sounds to be heard—perhaps only an occasional cry from the desert animals. The men of the Assyrian army were in deep sleep, unaware of the movement of the angel of the Lord. The angel was bringing God's judgment to the lives of 185,000 men of the Assyrian army.

The angel's actions were swift and well-planned. He left as swiftly as he had arrived. The silver moon began to fade; the first sound of the early morning birds awakened a few of the soldiers. If Sennacherib thought that he had problems the day before, he awakened this day to the biggest nightmare of his life!

Screams of woe were heard throughout the large army camp. Tent after tent was void of activity. As Sennacherib quickly dressed and rushed out to make an examination, he stumbled over dead bodies. The whole camp was awake now; dead bodies were being dragged out of tents by those still alive. The camp had been turned into a gigantic morgue. King Hezekiah no doubt watched from the high walls of Jerusalem and heard the eerie wails of the mourners. He watched, as did all his army and citizens, as the brave, boastful Assyrian army gathered up their weapons and fled in the direction of their Assyrian capital.

Sennacherib, whose name means "the moon god has increased brothers," was named after a moon god. But the true and living God Who made the sun and moon, sent a mighty angel who, in one night took the lives of 185,000 men—probably beneath the pale light of the moon.

Hezekiah means "Jehovah is strength"; and Hezekiah had trusted in the God Who is true to His name and reputation. The Lord had sent a mighty angel to display His strength against a proud, godless army.

Are you facing an "insurmountable" foe? Is there a problem in your life that looks unbeatable? God's mighty angels are more than adequate to handle any situation! Go to the house of the Lord, pray, seek godly prayer support in your time of need, and stand firm in your knowledge of the true God. The Lord will prove Himself to be the Almighty One over all the kingdoms of the earth—and over *your* particular problem too!

ANGELIC JUDGMENT UPON DAVID

There's something comforting about God sending His angels to judge unbelievers; we know that those who defy God deserve His judgment. But the Lord also uses angels to judge *believers* who violate God's laws. There is no partiality with God. Sin is sin, whether it is committed by unbelievers or believers; and God sometimes sends angels to carry out the sentence of judgment for disobedience. Such was the case with King David.

God had always fought for David. The Lord had always worked in the situations and circumstances of David's life through years of fighting against Israel's enemies. All of David's battles had been won—but they weren't won in David's strength alone. The victories always came because David and his men trusted in the God of Abraham, Isaac, and Jacob.

Toward the end of David's life, we read that Satan ''provoked'' him to take a census of Israel:

> *And Satan stood up against Israel, and provoked David to number Israel. And David said to Joab and to the rulers of the people, Go, number Israel from Beer-sheba even to Dan; and bring the number of them to me, that I may know it* (I Chronicles 21:1,2).

David evidently ceased trusting in the Lord. He wanted to trust in ''numbers'' rather than his God. David put his dependence upon a natural army instead of the supernatural power of God. David's desire to put his reliance upon the flesh was so great that he went against the sound counsel of his trusted friend Joab:

> *And Joab answered, The LORD make his people*

an hundred times so many more as they be: but, my lord the king, are they not all my lord's servants? why then doth my lord require this thing? why will he be a cause of trespass to Israel? (I Chronicles 21:3).

Many years later David's son Solomon would write, *For by wise counsel thou shalt make thy war: and in multitude of counsellors there is safety*" (Proverbs 24:6). David failed to take Joab's counsel; he left faith and got into flesh. God was not pleased:

And God was displeased with this thing; therefore he smote Israel (I Chronicles 21:7).

David had one thing in his favor, and I notice that this was always the case with David; he was fast to repent:

And David said unto God, I have sinned greatly, because I have done this thing: but now, I beseech thee, do away the iniquity of thy servant; for I have done very foolishly (I Chronicles 21:8).

God didn't have to wait very long for David's repentance, and David didn't try to shift the blame onto someone else as most of us do.

The Lord sent a prophet to David and offered him his choice of three different punishments. David had brought punishment upon the nation because of his sin, and God held the nation responsible for David's lapse. Why? I don't know, but maybe it was because they had failed to pray for their leader. We are commanded to pray for those in authority over us. Do *you* pray for our president, vice-president, legislators, and judges? As Christians, we have the responsibility to uphold our leaders and to pray that they exercise godly wisdom in all their decisions.

David could choose from three judgments: three years

of famine, fleeing three months before his enemies, or pestilence in the land for three days. David chose the pestilence. I think he was smart! Who wants three years of famine? Not me. And people can be cruel; David was smart to trust in God's mercy and take the pestilence.

An angel was dispatched to carry out God's judgment. This was the same type of angelic activity that destroyed 185,000 Assyrian troops. The angel began to execute God's sentence upon the people of Israel; but just as David must have known, God's mercy cut short the work of the angel:

> *And God sent an angel unto Jerusalem to destroy it: and as he was destroying, the LORD beheld, and he repented him of the evil, and said to the angel that destroyed, It is enough, stay now thine hand. And the angel of the LORD stood by the threshingfloor of Ornan the Jebusite* (I Chronicles 21:15).

The Bible says that David and the elders of Israel "fell upon their faces" when they saw the angel of the Lord. David took full responsibility for numbering the people. I think God liked that. David had a real shepherd's heart for the people; he didn't try to wiggle out of his sin. The Lord accepted David's repentance, and the angel gave David instructions concerning the construction of an altar so that David could offer a sacrifice:

> *Then the angel of the LORD commanded Gad to say to David, that David should go up, and set up an altar unto the LORD in the threshingfloor of Ornan the Jebusite* (I Chronicles 21:18).

David bought the threshing floor from Ornan, and God accepted his offering there by sending down fire to consume the sacrifice. All this happened on Mt. Moriah. Does that ring a bell? Mt. Moriah is where Abraham offered his son Isaac to the Lord. David offered a sacrifice on the same mountain. Many years later the Temple would be built on this site, and Jesus would be offered as a Sacrifice very near this spot!

What began as God's judgment was turned into a blessing because of repentance and the shedding of blood. God reversed the curse! And He can do the same thing for you. Has there been a place of sin in your life that has brought the judgment of God? God will certainly judge His people, but we can have the curse turned into blessings if we will repent and accept the shed blood of Jesus for our forgiveness. Angels can minister God's judgments upon us, or they can minister God's blessings upon us. The choice is up to us!

Chapter Nine

ANGELS IN YOUR FUTURE

I was too young to remember it, but my mother told me that my grandmother saw the glory of God just before she died. My mother was in the room when my grandmother died, and the sound of angels' wings was heard by those in the room.

You might ask, ''What do angels' wings have to do with someone dying?'' They have much to do with someone dying—if that person is a born-again Christian. Angels carry a believer's soul and spirit into the presence of God; they escort God's children from this earth to their heavenly abode.

Angels are our guardians while on this earth, and they are the ones who usher us into the presence of the Lord upon our death. How do we know that angels are heavenly ushers? We know it from the lips of Jesus Christ Himself. In Luke 16 we have Jesus' own account of two men who died. This is one of the few places in Scripture where the curtain is pulled back allowing us to see events which occur after death. Let's look first at the contrast our Lord makes between these two men while they were alive on earth:

> *There was a certain rich man, which was clothed in purple and fine linen, and fared sumptuously every day: And there was a certain beggar named Lazarus, which was laid at his gate, full of sores, And desiring to be fed with the crumbs which fell from the rich man's table: moreover the dogs came and licked his sores* (Luke 16:19-21).

Jesus told us about the rich man first. His diet included gourmet food every day. His clothing was the finest of linen; the color "purple" indicates that he was in the upper class. Outwardly this man seemed to have everything going for him. But as we shall see, it was his *inward* condition that determined his *eternal* residence.

In contrast to the rich man was Lazarus—a crippled beggar who had to be "laid" at the rich man's gate each day to beg for meager "crumbs" from the rich man's table. Lazarus was evidently so weak from malnutrition and sickness that he couldn't chase away the dogs who licked at his sores. Not a pretty sight!

In this life, the rich man had preeminence; even Jesus mentioned him first in this story. But in death, the order was reversed; and in death, we see the activity of angels in relation to the righteous:

> *And it came to pass, that the beggar died, and was carried by the angels into Abraham's bosom: the rich man also died, and was buried* (Luke 16:22).

Lazarus means "God has helped." Throughout Lazarus' lifetime, it looked as if he had no help. He was poor, crippled, and diseased. But Lazarus' help was manifested at death when God's angels came to help make his victorious passage into the presence of Jesus.

When the rich man died, Jesus simply said that he "was buried." There were no angels present to carry him to a heavenly reward. All his money, clothes, and fine foods couldn't stop the pull of sin that dragged him to hell:

> *And in hell he* [the rich man] *lift up his eyes, being in torments, and seeth Abraham afar off, and Lazarus in his bosom. And he cried and*

said, Father Abraham, have mercy on me, and send Lazarus, that he may dip the tip of his finger in water, and cool my tongue; for I am tormented in this flame (Luke 16:23,24).

Sin is a weight that pulls a person down. The sinner may look "on top of the world" in this life, but his true condition cannot be hidden from God. The writer to the Hebrews in the New Testament admonished his readers to . . . *lay aside every weight, and the sin which doth so easily beset us, . . .* " (Hebrews 12:1). The rich man "lived it up" while on earth, but his sin ultimately brought him down to hell.

What was the rich man's sin? Was it the fine clothes he wore? Or the sumptuous food he ate? Was it his wealth that kept the angels from carrying him into Abraham's bosom? No, Jesus indicated that the rich man's sin was in his failure to believe the Word of God. In Jesus' story the rich man asked Abraham to send Lazarus to speak with his relatives, warning them " . . . *lest they also come into this place of torment*" (Luke 16:28). Carefully observe Abraham's answer:

Abraham saith unto him, They have Moses and the prophets; let them hear them. And he said, Nay, father Abraham: but if one went unto them from the dead, they will repent. And he said unto him, If they hear not Moses and the prophets, neither will they be persuaded, though one rose from the dead (Luke 16:29-31).

The Scriptures alone are the infallible witness to the truth that God wants us to know and believe. Moses and the prophets all spoke of the coming Savior Who would die to take away man's sin. If we fail to believe what the

Bible says about the life, death, and resurrection of Jesus Christ, there will be no sound of angels' wings when we take our last breath.

Have *you* believed the gospel, the "good news" about Jesus' death for your sins? Are there angels in *your* future? If you're not sure, would you pray a short prayer with me? *"Dear God, I admit that I am a sinner who needs to be saved by Jesus Christ. I am sorry for my sin, and I confess the belief in my heart—according to the Bible—that Jesus Christ died for me, was resurrected from the dead, and now lives. I invite Your Holy Spirit to live in me and to make Jesus the Lord of my life. Thank You that at death I will be carried by Your angels to be in the presence of Jesus Christ. Amen."*

ANGELS AND PREPARATION FOR THIS LIFE

As we have seen throughout this book, angels are involved in *this* life as well as the life that is to come. Angels help prepare us for our life's work here on earth. Isaiah was a young prince in Israel when he had a dramatic encounter with an angel who came to prepare him for his future vocation:

> *In the year that king Uzziah died I saw also the Lord sitting upon a throne, high and lifted up, and his train filled the temple. Above it stood the seraphims: each one had six wings; with twain he covered his face, and with twain he covered his feet, and with twain he did fly* (Isaiah 6:1,2).

Isaiah's eyes were opened to a heavenly vision of the

Lord. This was at the time when Isaiah was about to begin his ministry as one of Israel's greatest prophets. Above the Lord's throne were seraphim—creatures with 6 wings. Seraphims seem to be associated with God's holiness. In Isaiah's vision, they may have been arranged in two rows as they cried out to one another concerning God's holy nature:

> *And one cried unto another, and said, Holy, holy, holy, is the* LORD *of hosts: the whole earth is full of his glory* (Isaiah 6:3).

When Isaiah saw the Lord and heard the seraphim, all he could think of was how *holy* the Lord was and how *unholy* he was:

> *Then said I, Woe is me! for I am undone; because I am a man of unclean lips,* . . . (Isaiah 6:5).

The seraphim bear some appearance to human beings because they are said to have faces, voices, feet, and hands. Now watch as one of these angelic beings prepares Isaiah for his life's work of speaking for God:

> *Then flew one of the seraphims unto me, having a live coal in his hand, which he had taken with the tongs from off the altar: And he laid it upon my mouth, and said, Lo, this hath touched thy lips; and thine iniquity is taken way, and thy sin purged* (Isaiah 6:6,7).

The angel took a coal off the brazen altar, which was where the lambs were sacrificed for the sin of the people. The angel took that coal and touched Isaiah's lips with it. The angel was saying, ''You have been cleansed so that you can speak God's words.''

After the seraphim prepared Isaiah for his future ministry, the Lord commissioned him:

> *Also I heard the voice of the Lord, saying, Whom shall I send, and who will go for us? Then said I, Here am I; send me. And he said, Go, and tell this people, Hear ye indeed, but understand not; and see ye indeed, but perceive not* (Isaiah 6:8,9).

Isaiah had first said, ''Woe''; the seraphim had said, ''Lo''; and now God said, ''Go!'' The angel had prepared Isaiah for his ministry by administering God's forgiveness and cleansing. Now Isaiah could *go forth* as God's prophet.

Eventually Isaiah would write 66 chapters of God's Word. Thirty-nine of those chapters are a miniature of the Old Testament which has 39 books, and 27 of Isaiah's chapters are a miniature of the New Testament which has 27 books. The first half of Isaiah's book speaks in images and warnings that coincide with the Old Testament message. The second half of Isaiah's book speaks of Jesus as the suffering Servant:

> *But he* [Jesus] *was wounded for our transgressions, he was bruised for our iniquities: the chastisement of our peace was upon him; and with his stripes we are healed* (Isaiah 53:5).

Isaiah had the greatest Old Testament revelation of Jesus. Why? Because Isaiah received the ministry of God's angel to prepare him for service and because he was obedient to God's call.

If you are a Christian, God has a special purpose for *your* life as well. The apostle Paul spoke of that *purpose* when he wrote a letter to the Christians at Rome:

> *And we know that all things work together for good to them that love God, to them who are the called according to his purpose* (Romans 8:28).

God has assigned His angels to help bring about the special purpose that He has for your life. Angels are "*. . . ministering spirits, sent forth to minister for them who shall be heirs of salvation*" (Hebrews 1:14). But you needn't wait for a spectacular vision like Isaiah's before you know what your "special purpose" is. ALL of us have been commissioned, like Isaiah, to "Go!" with the gospel of Jesus Christ. If you are a brand-new Christian, *go* to someone close to you and tell them of your new life in Christ. If you have been a Christian for any length of time, *go* to that neighbor or relative who hasn't heard the good news about forgiveness of sin through the death and resurrection of Christ. Remember, God's angels will go with you to minister to you *and* to those "*. . . who shall be heirs of salvation*"!

BELIEVERS WILL JUDGE ANGELS

The apostle Paul made a most interesting statement about angels in his letter to the believers at Corinth:

> *Dare any of you, having a matter against another, go to law before the unjust, and not before the saints? Do ye not know that the saints shall judge the world? and if the world shall be judged by you, are ye unworthy to judge the smallest matters? Know ye not that we shall judge angels? how much more things that pertain to this life?* (I Corinthians 6:1-3).

As wonderful as it is to be a Christian in *this* life, God has planned an even more marvelous future for us in the world to come! There is coming a time when the kingdoms of this world shall become the kingdoms of our Lord

(Revelation 11:15). And who do you think will be the administrators over those kingdoms? Daniel's prophecy makes it very clear that God's people will be the administrators:

> *But the saints of the most High shall take the kingdom, and possess the kingdom for ever, even for ever and ever. And the kingdom and dominion, and the greatness of the kingdom under the whole heaven, shall be given to the people of the saints of the most High, whose kingdom is an everlasting kingdom, and all dominions shall serve and obey him* (Daniel 7:18,27).

Jesus indicated that authority over cities will be given as a *reward* for those who have been faithful with what the Lord has given them to do in this world. This is brought out in His parable of the pounds:

> *And it came to pass, that when he was returned, having received the kingdom, then he commanded these servants to be called unto him, to whom he had given the money, that he might know how much every man had gained by trading. Then came the first, saying Lord, thy pound hath gained ten pounds. And he said unto him, Well, thou good servant: because thou hast been faithful in a very little, have thou authority over ten cities* (Luke 19:15-17).

The writer to the Hebrews made it very clear that it is *men* who will take part in governing the world to come:

> *For unto the angels hath he not put in subjection the world to come, whereof we speak. But one in a certain place testified, saying, What is man,*

> *that thou art mindful of him? or the son of man, that thou visitest him? Thou madest him a little lower than the angels; thou crownedst him with glory and honour, and didst set him over the works of thy hands: Thou hast put all things in subjection under his feet. For in that he put all in subjection under him, he left nothing that is not put under him. But now we see not yet all things put under him* (Hebrews 2:5-8).

You and I (as Christians) are to be part of God's *management* of the new heaven and the new earth. The initial part of that management includes participating in God's judgment upon the fallen angels. The little book of Jude in the New Testament tells us that God has already passed judgment upon some of the fallen angels:

> *And the angels which kept not their first estate, but left their own habitation, he hath reserved in everlasting chains under darkness unto the judgment of the great day* (Jude 6).

According to Paul's letter to the Corinthians, Christians will join in approving this final sentence of judgment upon the fallen angels. There certainly *are* angels in the future for believers and much more—we judge, rule, and reign with Christ!

ANGELS IN REVELATION

Have you ever been to Disneyland or Disney World? Each night there is a spectacular display of fireworks that lights up the sky. It's a fitting ending, and a grand finale, to anyone's stay in "The Magic Kingdom." The Bible is a book that takes us into the kingdom of God, and from

Genesis to Revelation we read about one particular class of inhabitants—the angels. But Revelation is truly God's *grand finale* of angelic activity, with 72 references to these dazzling, fascinating creatures!

Most of Revelation is concerned with future events. John divided his message into three parts:

> *Write the things which thou hast seen, and the things which are, and the things which shall be hereafter* (Revelation 1:19).

John had just finished seeing a vision of Jesus, and he was commanded to write it down. In chapters two and three, John recorded "the things which are" concerning seven local churches in his day. Finally, beginning in chapter four, John looked into the future where he recorded, in spectacular terms, the activities of angels—both good and bad angels. Let's take a look at a few of these angelic appearances that are in our future.

In chapter five of Revelation, we read about a book in the right hand of God, sealed with seven seals. This book is evidently the title deed of the earth, given to Adam by God. But Adam lost it to Satan through sin. As long as this book is sealed, Satan is in control of the earth. An angel by the throne asks an important question:

> *And I saw a strong angel proclaiming with a loud voice, Who is worthy to open the book, and to loose the seals thereof?* (Revelation 5:2).

John wept because he could see no one to open the title deed and reclaim the earth from Satan. Sometimes when we read the newspaper or watch TV, it certainly seems like this earth is firmly in the devil's grasp. But wait! John is told by an elder standing near the throne that there *is* Someone Who can open the book and reclaim the earth for God:

> *And one of the elders saith unto me, Weep not: behold, the Lion of the tribe of Juda, the Root of David, hath prevailed to open the book, and to loose the seven seals thereof* (Revelation 5:5).

Hallelujah! Don't give up on this old earth yet! Satan has done his best to corrupt it and the people in it, but there is coming a day when the kingdoms of this world will become the kingdoms of our Lord. The book of Revelation gives us a glimpse of that day.

ANGELS SEAL THE 144,000

In chapter seven of Revelation we read about four angels who hold back the winds of judgment that are about to be unleashed upon the earth:

> *And after these things I saw four angels standing on the four corners of the earth, holding the four winds of the earth, that the wind should not blow on the earth, nor on the sea, nor on any tree* (Revelation 7:1).

Some people think that God made the earth and then left it to run on its own—like a giant watch that is wound up and then left to run down. But that is not what the Bible teaches! God is involved in every part of our lives and in every aspect of life on earth. His angels help control even the weather. Job was reminded of God's sovereignty over the forces of nature when the Lord answered him out of the whirlwind:

> *Hast thou entered into the treasures of the snow? or hast thou seen the treasures of the hail, Which I have reserved against the time of trouble, against the day of battle and war? By what way*

is the light parted, which scattereth the east wind upon the earth? (Job 38:22-24).

Our God controls the snow, the hail, the lightning, the rain, and the wind. One day soon His angels will unleash the mighty forces of nature in judgment upon an unbelieving world. During this time spoken of in Revelation, overcoming believers will have been raptured. But God will still have a people on the earth who need His divine protection from judgment. An angel will see to it that those who belong to God are saved from the wrath to come:

And I saw another angel ascending from the east, having the seal of the living God; and he cried with a loud voice to the four angels, to whom it was given to hurt the earth and the sea, Saying, Hurt not the earth, neither the sea, nor the trees, till we have sealed the servants of our God in their forehead (Revelation 7:2,3).

God's people are afforded protection in His time of judgment just as Lot was protected from the destruction of Sodom and Gomorrah. The seal could be the outpouring of the Holy Spirit:

And Jesus, when he was baptized, went up straightway out of the water: and, lo, the heavens were opened unto him, and he saw the Spirit of God descending like a dove, and lighting upon him (Matthew 3:16).

Labour not for the meat which perisheth, but for that meat which endureth unto everlasting life, which the Son of man shall give unto you: for him hath God the Father sealed (John 6:27).

In whom ye also trusted, after that ye heard the

word of truth, the gospel of your salvation: in whom also after that ye believed, ye were sealed with the Holy Spirit of promise (Ephesians 1:13).

Have you been sealed? Have you received that "Holy Spirit of promise"? You do not have to fear the judgments that will come upon the earth if you have repented of your sins and asked Jesus Christ to be the Lord of your life. If you are a born-again Christian, God's angels have been assigned to you for your protection:

Because thou hast made the LORD, which is my refuge, even the most High, thy habitation; There shall no evil befall thee, neither shall any plague come nigh thy dwelling. For he shall give his angels charge over thee, to keep thee in all thy ways. They shall bear thee up in their hands, lest thou dash thy foot against a stone (Psalms 91:9-12).

JESUS: THE MIGHTY ANGEL

The book mentioned in Revelation 5 is seen again in chapter 10, only this time the book is in the hand of a "mighty angel":

And I saw another mighty angel come down from heaven, clothed with a cloud: and a rainbow was upon his head, and his face was as it were the sun, and his feet as pillars of fire: And he had in his hand a little book open: and he set his right foot upon the sea, and his left foot on the earth (Revelation 10:1,2).

This "mighty angel" is undoubtedly Jesus Christ. Compare His description here with the description of

Christ found in the first chapter of Revelation:

> *His head and his hairs were white like wool, as white as snow; and his eyes were as a flame of fire; And his feet like unto fine brass, as if they burned in a furnace; and his voice as the sound of many waters. And he had in his right hand seven stars: and out of his mouth went a sharp two-edged sword: and his countenance was as the sun shineth in his strength* (Revelation 1:14-16).

Remember, too, that earlier in Revelation we read where Jesus was coming "with clouds" (Revelation 1:7). And Jesus had told the disciples that all the tribes of the earth would see the Son of Man coming in the clouds (Matthew 24:30). In the book of Exodus, God the Father is seen as clothed with a cloud (Exodus 40:34-38 and Leviticus 16:2). Only deity is said to be "clothed with a cloud."

Another indication that this mighty angel is Jesus Christ is found in Revelation 10:

> *And cried with a loud voice, as when a lion roareth:* . . . (Revelation 10:3).

Jesus was described as the Lion of Judah in Revelation 5:5. And of course, Jesus is also described as the "Sun" in the Old Testament:

> *But unto you that fear my name shall the Sun of righteousness arise with healing in his wings;* . . . (Malachi 4:2).

ANGELIC FIREWORKS

Satan and the fallen angels, who followed him in his rebellion against God, are presently dwelling in the *heavenlies* (not God's *heaven*, but the space above the earth). The time will soon come when they will be displaced from the heavenlies to the earth to fiercely persecute those who are saved during the coming Great Tribulation. Satan was cast out of God's heaven as his *dwelling* place long ago. However, he still has *access* to heaven until a future time.

The permanent expulsion of Satan and his angels from heaven is described in Revelation 12:7-9:

> *And there was war in heaven: Michael and his angels fought against the dragon; and the dragon fought and his angels, And prevailed not; neither was their place found any more in heaven. And the great dragon was cast out, that old serpent, called the Devil, and Satan, which deceiveth the whole world: he was cast out into the earth, and his angels were cast out with him* (Revelation 12:7-9).

Many times in Scripture, angels are referred to as "stars" (see Isaiah 14:12 and Revelation 12:4). Thus the Bible described "Star Wars" long before man used the term!

Who is "Michael" mentioned in Revelation 12:7? He is the leader of God's angelic forces:

> *And at that time shall Michael stand up, the great prince which standeth for the children of thy people: and there shall be a time of trouble, such as never was since there was a nation even to that same time: . . .* (Daniel 12:1).

Michael, as leader of God's angelic hosts, will come against the devil and his angels. What a battle that will be! But God's Word assures us that the devil and his angels "prevailed not" against God's heavenly warriors. Satan will be "cast down" to earth where he will begin his persecution of God's people during the Tribulation period.

Imagine Satan's fury against the believers on earth at this time. But as we have seen, God's people are ''sealed'' and protected and equipped to overcome the devil. Verse 11 of chapter 12 tells us how the Christians overcome the attacks of this fallen angel:

> *And they overcame him by the blood of the Lamb, and by the word of their testimony; and they loved not their lives unto the death* (Revelation 12:11).

Their first line of defense is the ''blood of the Lamb.'' As believers in the death and resurrection of Jesus Christ, they can speak the Word of God with authority. The apostle James said that believers should '' . . . *Resist the devil, and he will flee from you*'' (James 4:7). The way to resist is to speak the Word with the authority that only comes from accepting the shed blood of Jesus on your behalf.

There is more to the Christian life, however, than merely overcoming the devil and his angels. Believers are called to do mighty exploits for the Lord. Can we do these alone? Of course not; and that is why in our final chapter we are going to learn how to *activate our angels* to help us walk in God's fullness!

Chapter Ten

ACTIVATE YOUR ANGELS

It's one thing to know that there are thousands of angels who are ready and willing to minister to us and for us, and quite another thing to put them into action! Don't let those hosts of angels sit around all day eating manna—put them to work! I put my angels to work every morning; I picture angels surrounding my husband, children, and grandchildren. I pray that God will encompass Happy Church and Marilyn Hickey Ministries with angels who will keep us in all our ways.

As I pray, I see those angels around my daughter's car; I see them sitting on the fender and on the bumper. I even see them (in my mind) holding onto the door handles!

You may think, "Oh, Marilyn, isn't that going a bit too far?" No, not at all! I know by faith that they are there; and with the eye of faith, I see them at their assigned posts.

When I travel, I visualize angels covering the airplane. I picture them on the wings, the tail, and with the pilot. I know that angels go before me and after me.

If fear tries to grip me when I am home alone, I visualize God's angels around our house. In faith I see them at the back and front doors and at every window. I have complete peace and confidence that my angels are working around the clock for me.

We are protected by an elite angelic force. The Bible says that the angel of the Lord *encamps* around those who fear God (Psalms 34:7). Do *you* fear God? Do you regard Him with deep love, respect, and awe? Then you have an angelic encampment surrounding you!

SPECIAL DELIVERY!

We have seen how angels are God's messengers; sometimes the word *angel* is even used of human beings who act as God's messengers. I believe that God used a human messenger to answer the prayers of a frantic housewife.

Let's call her Ruth. Her name doesn't really matter, but what mattered was that she was out of laundry detergent! She and her husband and infant were barely making it from paycheck to paycheck. Early one Saturday morning she gathered up laundry—only to find that she was out of detergent. Most of the items could wait, but she just *had* to have clean diapers for her baby.

''Lord,'' she prayed, ''You know I need detergent. I don't know how You're going to do it, but I'm praying that somehow I'll have money for detergent.''

It wasn't long before she heard a noise at the front door. When she investigated it, there was a sample of laundry detergent hanging on her doorknob! Praise the Lord! The person who had hung it there was probably unaware of being used as God's messenger to answer one woman's prayer. But that little incident reaffirmed to Ruth God's care for even the smallest needs in our lives.

ACTIVATING *YOUR* ANGELS

Are you thinking, ''Well, Marilyn, you say that angels encamp around those who fear the Lord. *I* fear the Lord and I love the Lord, but where are the angels who are supposed to be working for me? I haven't noticed them doing anything.''

If your angels aren't active, don't despair! There is a way to activate your angels, and David spells it out in one of the psalms:

> *Bless the* L*ORD, ye his angels, that excel in strength, that do his commandments, hearkening unto the voice of his word* (Psalms 103:20).

David said that angels move at the command of God's Word. We have already seen how angels were involved in the judgment upon Sodom and Gomorrah, but the other side of that judgment is seen in the way Abraham activated his angels on behalf of his loved ones.

All of us have loved ones who need the intervention of God's angels on their behalf. The Lord wants *us* to be involved in that intervention. We can't just sit back and say, "Well, God's angels will do it all. I don't have to do anything; God will do it all."

That's lazy Christianity! If you're a Christian, then the Word is in you; and if the Word is in you, you'll be working instead of sitting around and wishing for something to happen out of the blue.

We are going to look at how Abraham activated his angels, and we are going to be encouraged to do the same thing for our loved ones and for ourselves. Don't think that angelic activity is for someone else, someone more spiritual than you. God has plenty of angels to go around, and there are plenty of them just waiting for you to set them to work through speaking God's Word to them.

The book of Hebrews says that some have entertained angels unawares (Hebrews 13:2), but Abraham seemed to have been very aware of the angels he was entertaining:

> *And he* [Abraham] *lift up his eyes and looked, and lo, three men stood by him: and when*

> *he saw them, he ran to meet them from the tent door, and bowed himself toward the ground* (Genesis 18:2).

These weren't ordinary visitors. The Bible says that one of the three men was actually the Lord! A meal was prepared, and Abraham and Sarah were promised a son in their old age. The three men said their goodbyes and began the walk toward Sodom and Gomorrah. But before they left Abraham, the Lord decided to let him in on a secret:

> *And the LORD said, Shall I hide from Abraham that thing which I do; For I know him, that he will command his children and his household after him, and they shall keep the way of the LORD, to do justice and judgment; that the LORD may bring upon Abraham that which he hath spoken of him* (Genesis 18:17,19).

Did you notice what *our* part is? If we are to have God working on our behalf, we need to command our children and our household to follow the Lord. We must "do justice and judgment." Are we just in all our affairs? Do we use proper judgment concerning our everyday activities? Then what can we expect? We can expect God to bring upon us all the promises of His Word—including the ministry of angels.

Verses 22 and 23 are the key to activating angels:

> *And the men turned their faces from thence, and went toward Sodom: but Abraham stood yet before the LORD. And Abraham drew near, and said, Wilt thou also destroy the righteous with the wicked?* (Genesis 18:22,23).

To Whom was Abraham talking? The Lord. What was

Abraham doing? He was vigorously interceding for his loved ones. Abraham heard that God was going to destroy the towns of Sodom and Gomorrah, and he immediately thought of Lot, Lot's wife and daughters, and their husbands. What was Abraham doing here? He was reasoning in prayer with God:

> *Peradventure there be fifty righteous within the city: wilt thou also destroy and not spare the place for the fifty righteous that are therein? That be far from thee to do after this manner, to slay the righteous with the wicked: and that the righteous should be as the wicked, that be far from thee: Shall not the Judge of all the earth do right?* (Genesis 18:24,25).

Abraham didn't give up praying until he got God's promise to spare the city of Sodom if there were only ten righteous. Do you think that you and I can pray to God like that? Can we reason with the Lord in the same way? Yes! We can pray for our loved ones based upon God's own Word:

> *Though hand join in hand, the wicked shall not be unpunished: but the seed of the righteous shall be delivered* (Proverbs 11:21).
>
> *And they said, Believe on the Lord Jesus Christ, and thou shalt be saved, and thy house* (Acts 16:31).

These are just two of the most well-known promises for household salvation. How do you activate angels? By praying God's own Word to Him. Remember, angels hearken to God's Word. If we're praying our own words, our own opinions of what we want, we can't expect angels to move an inch. They don't move at *our* words; they move upon *the* Word!

Many times when we are faced with a problem or a "hopeless" situation, we *pray the problem.* By that I mean that we focus in on the problem; we get on the phone and rehash the problem to everybody we can think of. Problem, problem, problem. That's all we can think about or talk about. But problems don't bring answers or provisions; *promises bring provisions.* Praying God's *answers* brings God's *angels.*

Someone has said that there are over 7,000 promises in the Bible. What does God want to hear from you when you pray? He wants to hear the promise that matches your problem. When you pray the promise, angels move at the command of God's Word.

Abraham had prayed for Lot. The Lord had said that He would not destroy Sodom if He could find ten righteous people. Now it was time for the angels to act upon God's Word:

> *And there came two angels to Sodom at even; and Lot sat in the gate of Sodom: and Lot seeing them rose up to meet them; and he bowed himself with his face toward the ground* (Genesis 19:1).

The angels went to Lot. Why? Because Abraham had prayed for his loved ones. Do you want angels to minister to your loved ones? Then pray God's Word for them. Along with your prayers, keep your own house in divine order. Notice the reluctance of the angels to enter into Lot's house:

> *And he said, Behold now, my lords, turn in, I pray you, into your servant's house, and tarry all night, and wash your feet, and ye shall rise up early, and go on your ways. And they*

> *said, Nay; but we will abide in the street all night* (Genesis 19:2).

Do you remember how these same angels were eager to eat with Abraham? What was the difference? The difference was that Abraham's house was filled with justice and good judgment. Lot's house had an ungodly atmosphere. If we don't command our houses in the Word of God, we are not going to have the angelic activity we would like to have.

Abraham had asked the Lord to spare the city if ten righteous people were in it. When it came right down to it, only Lot, his wife, and their two daughters were spared. Notice the Lord's mercy and the angelic activity that was the answer to Abraham's prayer:

> *And when the morning arose, then the angels hastened Lot, saying, Arise, take thy wife, and thy two daughters, which are here; lest thou be consumed in the iniquity of the city. And while he lingered, the men laid hold upon his hand, and upon the hand of his wife, and upon the hand of his two daughters: the LORD being merciful unto him: and they brought him forth, and set him without the city* (Genesis 19:15,16).

Lot certainly didn't deserve to be rescued, but God was merciful. Why was God merciful? Why did God send angels to Lot? Because Abraham prayed. What made the difference? What initiated the ministry of angels on Lot's behalf? Prayer! Abraham rescued Lot by prayer.

Abraham could have thought to himself, "Lot never should have moved down there in the first place. He got himself into this trouble; now he can just try to get himself out." But Abraham was compassionate, and I think God liked Abraham's attitude.

Are there some members of your family who look like hopeless cases? Are there some people who look to be too far into sin to be rescued? Stop looking at their condition and start praying the promises of God. Your faith can make the difference in their lives. God will send forth His angels to minister to them if you, like Abraham, will intercede.

THE PRAYER THAT BROUGHT AN ANGEL

I think that some angels are just plain bored with the Christians to whom they are assigned because those Christians are never active in the Word. Some Christians never see their faith fired into action because they don't pray. Praying God's word unleashes His angels to perform the supernatural.

Two of the dearest prayer warriors I have ever met are Mark and Huldah Buntain—the couple whose orphanage, church, and hospital in Calcutta, India, have helped thousands of people to live better lives and to find the Savior. God has proven Himself faithful to them in their 25-plus years in one of the poorest areas on earth; and now that Mark has gone on to be with the Lord, Huldah continues to carry on the much-needed work.

Before his death, Mark had an unusual encounter with an angel that I want to share with you. After many years of hard work to establish their ministry in Calcutta, terrible rains caused so much flooding that the government ordered an evacuation of much of the city.

As he boarded an evacuation plane, Mark was troubled by what was to become of the work he and Huldah had started. Would the flooding wipe away the orphanage and church they had worked so hard to build? Would they have to start all over? Discouragement started to creep into Mark's mind as he sat staring out the plane's window. He sat alone and prayed for the people of Calcutta and for the work God had called them to do.

Another passenger sat down next to Mark and began to talk with him as the plane took off. The stranger began talking about India's future and encouraged Mark to continue in his work. The man even outlined several steps Mark and Huldah could take to make their work more effective!

Although Mark said he didn't know the man and had never seen him before, faith began rising in his spirit and he felt new direction and encouragement from the Lord. A short while later a stewardess caught his attention and asked if he would like something to drink. He ordered for himself and turned to speak to the man beside him—but he was gone!

Mark thought that surely the man must be somewhere else on the small plane, but a search for him revealed nothing. Mark even asked the stewardess if she had seen the man, but she had not. It was then that Mark realized he had been visited by an angel.

When the floodwaters receded and the Buntains returned to their work, the things shared by the stranger proved to be a great help. Mark never forgot that encounter (how could he?), and he never forgot how God's encouragement and guidance had come from one of God's angelic messengers as the result of prayer.

ANGELS, PRAYER, AND MONEY

You certainly can't buy an angelic visitation; but if you

want angels to be active in your life, you must be a person of prayer and a person who gives. There was just such a person in the days of the apostle Peter; his name was Cornelius. You can read about his angelic visitation in the tenth chapter of the New Testament book of Acts:

> *There was a certain man in Caesarea called Cornelius, a centurion of the band called the Italian band, A devout man, and one that feared God with all his house, which gave much alms to the people, and prayed to God alway* (Acts 10:1.2).

Angels are active in the lives of those who pray and who give; Cornelius wasn't holding anything back from God. If the Lord has your pocketbook, He has your heart! Cornelius had a heart that was turned totally toward God. As a result, this gentile soldier had an angelic visitation:

> *He saw in a vision evidently about the ninth hour of the day an angel of God coming in to him, and saying unto him, Cornelius. And when he looked on him, he was afraid, and said, What is it, Lord? And he said unto him, Thy prayers and thine alms are come up for a memorial before God* (Acts 10:3,4).

Notice what comes before God: your prayers *and* your giving. Cornelius was building something in heaven. What was it? He was building a *memorial*. Some people like to make a big name for themselves on earth; they may even have a building or two named after them. But in time those buildings will become old and crumble. Cornelius was building something with his prayers and his giving that would last eternally. God saw the memorial Cornelius was building, and He sent His angel to guide and direct

Cornelius into the fullness of the Holy Spirit:

> *And now send men to Joppa, and call for one Simon, whose surname is Peter: He lodgeth with one Simon a tanner, whose house is by the sea side: he shall tell thee what thou oughtest to do* (Acts 10:5,6).

Cornelius would be the first gentile filled with the Holy Spirit. Up until this time the Church was composed of Jews and Jewish proselytes. Peter had the Word of God for Cornelius that would shake the Church and open the floodgates for gentiles everywhere. Why do you suppose God singled out Cornelius? Because he prayed and he gave!

Don't overlook what took place next in the life of Cornelius:

> *And when the angel which spake unto Cornelius was departed, he called two of his household servants, and a devout soldier of them that waited on him continually: And when he had declared all these things unto them, he sent them to Joppa* (Acts 10:7,8).

What did Cornelius do when his angelic visitation was over? He *obeyed* the message brought by the angel. Angels are *messengers*, not *entertainers*. Their work is serious and their messages are the very words of God. *Obedience* is the proper response to an angelic visitation. Because of his obedience, Cornelius is mentioned by name in our Bible. And because of his obedience, Cornelius received God's gift of the Holy Spirit:

> *While Peter yet spake these words, the Holy Ghost fell on all them which heard the word. And they of the circumcision which believed were astonished, as many as came with Peter, because*

> *that on the Gentiles also was poured out the gift of the Holy Ghost* (Acts 10:44,45).

God has many gifts for you as well. Whatever needs are in your life can be overcome through the Word, through prayer, and through the giving of yourself and your finances. God has assigned angels to minister *to* you and *for* you; they are all around you. The time has come for you to activate *your* angels.

Pray this prayer with me, and together let's make the commitment necessary to see miraculous angelic activity in our personal lives, in our families, our finances, our health, and in every other area of our lives:

Dear heavenly Father, I come to You in the mighty name of Jesus. I confess that my angels have been idle too long. I desire to be a person who is saturated with Your Word, a person who is continually in prayer, and a person who is looking for more ways to give of all that You have given me. Beginning today, I will pray Your promises for my every need; and I believe that Your angels will move to fulfill Your Word. Thank you, Father, for Your angelic ministry to me. In Jesus' name, amen.

BIBLIOGRAPHY

Capps, Charles. ANGELS. Tulsa: Harrison House, 1984.

Graham, Billy. ANGELS: GOD'S SECRET AGENTS. New York: Doubleday & Company, Inc., 1975.

Lindsay, Gordon. MINISTRY OF ANGELS. Dallas: Christ for the Nations, Inc., 1979.

Shaw, Gwen. OUR MINISTERING ANGELS. Jasper, Arkansas: Engeltal Press, 1986.

Sumrall, Lester. THE REALITY OF ANGELS. South Bend, Indiana: LeSEA Publishing Company, Inc., 1982.

Receive Jesus Christ as Lord and Savior of Your Life.

The Bible says, "That if thou shalt confess with thy mouth the Lord Jesus, and shalt believe in thine heart that God hath raised him from the dead, thou shalt be saved. For with the heart man believeth unto righteousness; and with the mouth confession is made unto salvation" (Romans 10:9,10).

To receive Jesus Christ as Lord and Savior of your life, sincerely pray this prayer from your heart:

Dear Jesus,

I believe that You died for me and that You rose again on the third day. I confess to You that I am a sinner and that I need Your love and forgiveness. Come into my life, forgive my sins, and give me eternal life. I confess You now as my Lord. Thank You for my salvation!

Signed ______________________________

Date ______________________________

Write to us.

We will send you information to help you with your new life in Christ.

Marilyn Hickey Ministries • P.O. Box 17340
Denver, CO 80217 • (303) 770-0400

For Your Information

Free Monthly Magazine

☐ Please send me your free monthly magazine OUTPOURING (including daily devotionals, timely articles, and ministry updates)!

Tapes and Books

☐ Please send me Marilyn's latest product catalog.

Name Mr. & Mrs. / Miss / Mrs. / Mr. ______________________________
Please Print

Address ______________________________

City ______________________________

State ____________________ Zip ______________

Phone (H) (____) ______________________________

(W) (____) ______________________________

Mail to
Marilyn Hickey Ministries
P.O. Box 17340
Denver, CO 80217

Prayer Requests

Let us join our faith with yours for your prayer needs. Fill out below and send to

Marilyn Hickey Ministries
P.O. Box 17340
Denver, CO 80217

Prayer Request ____

____

____

____

____

____

Name Mr. & Mrs. / Mr. / Miss / Mrs. ____

Address ____

City ____

State ______________________________ Zip ______________

Phone (H) (   ) ______________________________

(W) (   ) ______________________________

☐ If you want prayer immediately, call our Prayer Center at (303) 796-1333, 24 hours per day, 7 days a week.

BOOKS BY MARILYN HICKEY

A CRY FOR MIRACLES ($5.95)
ACTS ($7.95)
ANGELS ALL AROUND ($7.95)
BEAT TENSION ($.75)
BIBLE CAN CHANGE YOU, THE ($12.95)
BOLD MEN WIN ($.75)
BREAK THE GENERATION CURSE ($7.95)
BULLDOG FAITH ($.75)
CHANGE YOUR LIFE ($.75)
CHILDREN WHO HIT THE MARK ($.75)
CONQUERING SETBACKS ($.75)
DAILY DEVOTIONAL ($5.95)
DEAR MARILYN ($5.95)
DIVORCE IS NOT THE ANSWER ($4.95)
ESPECIALLY FOR TODAY'S WOMAN ($14.95)
EXPERIENCE LONG LIFE ($.75)
FASTING & PRAYER ($.75)
FREEDOM FROM BONDAGES ($4.95)
GIFT-WRAPPED FRUIT ($2.00)
GOD'S BENEFIT: HEALING ($.75)
GOD'S COVENANT FOR YOUR FAMILY ($5.95)
GOD'S RX FOR A HURTING HEART ($3.50)
GOD'S SEVEN KEYS TO MAKE YOU RICH ($.75)
HOLD ON TO YOUR DREAM ($.75)
HOW TO BECOME A MATURE CHRISTIAN ($5.95)
HOW TO BECOME MORE THAN A CONQUEROR ($.75)
HOW TO WIN FRIENDS ($.75)
I CAN BE BORN AGAIN AND SPIRIT FILLED ($.75)
I CAN DARE TO BE AN ACHIEVER ($.75)
KEYS TO HEALING REJECTION ($.75)
KNOW YOUR MINISTRY ($3.50)
MAXIMIZE YOUR DAY . . . GOD'S WAY ($7.95)
NAMES OF GOD ($7.95)
#1 KEY TO SUCCESS—MEDITATION ($3.50)
POWER OF FORGIVENESS, THE ($.75)
POWER OF THE BLOOD, THE ($.75)
RECEIVING RESURRECTION POWER ($.75)
RENEW YOUR MIND ($.75)
SATAN-PROOF YOUR HOME ($7.95)
"SAVE THE FAMILY" PROMISE BOOK ($14.95)
SIGNS IN THE HEAVENS ($4.95)
SOLVING LIFE'S PROBLEMS ($.75)
SPEAK THE WORD ($.75)
STANDING IN THE GAP ($.75)
STORY OF ESTHER, THE ($.75)
WINNING OVER WEIGHT ($.75)
WOMEN OF THE WORD ($.75)
YOUR MIRACLE SOURCE ($3.50)
YOUR PERSONALITY WORKOUT ($5.95)